The
LOBSTER
COOKBOOK

The
LOBSTER
COOKBOOK

55 easy recipes: bisques, noodles, salads, soups, bakes, wraps, grills and fries for every day eating

JANE BAMFORTH

LORENZ BOOKS

CONTENTS

INTRODUCTION 6

Lobster for all 8

Lobsters 10

Crabs 12

Prawns and shrimp 14

Crayfish and langoustines 15

Equipment 16

Buying, preparing and cooking
   large shellfish 18

Sauces for shellfish 26

SOUPS AND BISQUES 30

APPETIZERS 48

SALADS, BURGERS AND BITES 60

PASTA, RICE AND NOODLES 74

FIRES AND GRILLS 90

**BAKES, STEWS AND STEAMED
   DISHES 108**

Index 126

INTRODUCTION

Considered to be the king of shellfish, lobster is a
delicacy that is enjoyed at top restaurants all over the
world. Happily, fresh and frozen sustainable lobster is
now readily available at a price that means you can
enjoy it for a quick snack, a filling mid-week supper as
well as an impressive dinner party dish.

LOBSTER FOR ALL

Lobster is often considered to be the king of shellfish and was traditionally an expensive delicacy only enjoyed at top restaurants by those who could afford it. Nowadays, very reasonably priced, prepared whole lobster is readily available from most supermarkets, fishmongers and online suppliers, meaning it has increased enormously in popularity for home cooks. Much more affordable lobster dishes are also offered at many restaurants now.

The increase in availability of lobster, and the resulting decrease in price, is due to several factors. The rise in sea temperature, due to climate change, has led to a longer lobster growing season – they are hatching earlier and growing quicker. Over-fishing in the Atlantic has also depleted the stocks of cod, which prey on baby lobsters, resulting in more fully-developed lobsters in Canadian and US waters.

The unique, delicious sweet flavour and firm meaty texture of lobster makes it a great choice for a wide range of dishes. There are also health benefits to eating lobster as it is low in fat, high in protein and rich in potassium, calcium, phosphorus, magnesium and sodium, with significant amounts of vitamin A, E, B6 and choline. It is also rich in healthy omega-3 fatty acids. It does also contain cholesterol although recent studies have suggested the cholesterol content in food does not necessarily increase harmful cholesterol in the body.

If you've never cooked lobster before it's best to start with frozen. Lobsters are frozen raw or cooked, so no need to worry about killing a live lobster. Frozen ready-cooked lobster simply needs to be defrosted and then the meat extracted. These are the best choice when ready-cooked lobster meat is specified in a recipe such as Lobster Cakes with Tartare Sauce (page 51) or Lobster Bisque (page 32). Lobsters that have been frozen uncooked need to be thawed and then cooked whole – these can be used in place of live lobster in a recipe such as Grilled Lobster with Tarragon Cream (page 92).

An alternative way to buy lobster is to choose fresh or frozen lobster tails. These meaty tails only take a few minutes to steam, with some fresh herbs and lemon or lime slices, and the shell just needs to be peeled off before serving. The cooked tails can be served simply with a drizzle of melted butter and lemon juice or with a sauce. Alternatively, the meat can be added to pasta or used in sandwiches, wraps, salads and risottos.

If you prefer to cook live lobster rather than frozen, where do you start? How do you go about buying and preparing it – after all those sharp pincers can appear quite

Above: Live lobsters are now more easily available from online suppliers.

Opposite: Distinctive lobster nets stacked on the quay will mean fresh local shellfish should be easy to find.

daunting. Traditionally, the only way to buy lobster was to choose a whole live lobster (supplied with rubber bands to secure the pincers). The lobster was then chilled to humanely render it oblivious before simply boiling it. This is still the best way to prepare fresh lobster (see page 19). Preparing and cooking a live lobster at home used to be very much dependent on having a good fishmonger nearby or living within easy distance of the sea where lobsters were regularly landed by the local fisherman. However, live lobster is now available from a range of online fish suppliers – the lobsters are supplied live after chilling but should be used as soon as possible (do check the specific storage timings with the supplier). And as for the pincers, the best way to make sure you don't get nipped is to always leave the bands on their claws – lobsters are carnivorous so the bands prevent them from attacking and eating each other as they are very strong and fast, and also from having a go at you, too (this will only happen at room temperature).

As an alternative to lobster there are a variety of recipes in this book using other crustaceans that also have sweet, meaty flesh, such as crab, crayfish, langoustine and prawns. These are readily available and are also delicious. Choose from a selection of soups, salads and main courses as well as barbecue ideas.

From details about the different types of lobster to basic preparation and cooking techniques together with a whole range of delicious recipes there's something here to suit all cooks and once you've enjoyed it at home, you'll be surprised at just how versatile lobster is.

LOBSTERS

With their firm, sweet flesh and delicious flavour many people regard lobsters as the finest crustaceans of all. The best-tasting lobsters live in cold ocean waters, scavenging for food on the rocky sea bed. Like crabs, they 'moult' every couple of years, casting off their outgrown shells and forming a new one. Their colour varies according to their habitat, from steely blue or greenish-brown to reddish-purple, but all lobsters turn a bright brick red when they are cooked. Lobsters grow very slowly, only reaching maturity at six years old, by which time they are approximately 18cm/7in long. If you are lucky enough to find a 1kg/2¼lb sized lobster, it will be around ten years old.

COLD-WATER LOBSTERS

The cold-water lobster has a sweeter and juicier flavour than its warm-water counterpart. Cold-water lobsters also have a pair of claws – the larger claw has wide teeth for crushing its prey, the second claw is smaller and has sharp teeth for

Right: Maine lobster resembles the European lobster, but is less expensive.

ripping flesh. These lobsters live in the waters of the North Atlantic and there are two main types – the American variety can be found as far south as South Carolina, while the European lobster's habitat extends from the far north down to the Mediterranean. Cold-water lobsters can also be found in the oceans off South Africa, New Zealand and Australia.

CANADIAN/AMERICAN LOBSTER
(Homarus americanus)

The hardiest species of lobster, these are found in large numbers in the waters around Canada and the Northern American Atlantic. They resemble the European lobster, but are greener in colour, and the claws are slightly rounder and fleshier. Although they make excellent eating, their flavour does not quite match up to that of the European species.

The best-known American lobster is the Maine lobster.

EUROPEAN LOBSTER
(Homarus gammarus)

These lobsters, which come from the waters of England, Scotland, Ireland, Norway and Brittany, are regarded as having the finest flavour of all. They have distinctive blue-black colouring, and are sometimes speckled with bright blue. European lobsters are more rare and expensive than their North American counterparts.

In France a lobster is called an homard; in Italy it is astice; and in Spain bogavante.

WARM-WATER LOBSTERS

Strictly speaking, the warm-water crustaceans that are usually referred to as lobsters are not actually lobsters. They are also sometimes called spiny lobsters or rock lobsters. They have a fishier and less sweet meat than cold-water lobsters. They are found in the warm waters of California, Brazil and the Caribbean and are generally harvested just for their meaty tails.

Left: Warm-water lobsters have long antennae but no claws.

The easiest way to tell if a lobster is from cold or warm water is to see if it has claws – warm-water lobsters do not. Instead of using claws to crush the shell of molluscs, they use their mandibles (jawbone). They have harder shells than cold-water lobsters and very long antennae.

CRAWFISH

(Palinurus vulgaris)

Similar to lobsters, warm water crawfish have spiny shells and no claws. They are sometimes also known as crayfish but must not be confused with freshwater crayfish. Crawfish are found on the rocky sea bed in many parts of the world. Atlantic crawfish, from Brazil, are dark reddish-brown; those from the Florida coast are brown with pale spots; some varieties can be pink or bluish-green. All turn pink or red when cooked.

Crawfish have dense, very white flesh, similar to that of lobster, but with a milder flavour. Those from the Atlantic are the sweetest. In France, crawfish are called langouste; in Italy they are aragosta; in Spain langosta.

Crawfish are generally sold cooked. Females have the best flavour, so look for the egg sac underneath the thorax. Because there is no claw meat, allow 450g/1lb per person. Florida crawfish are often sold frozen as 'lobster' tails.

SLIPPER/SQUAT LOBSTER

(Scyllarus arctus)

There are over fifty species of these warm water lobsters. They have wide, flattened bodies and spindly, clawed legs. The best known squat lobsters are the Australian 'bugs', and the best known of these are the Balmain and Moreton Bay bugs. The comparatively small tails contain deliciously sweet flesh. Squat lobsters are seldom sold in Europe, but can occasionally be found in France, where they are known as cigales (grasshoppers). Italians call them cicala di mare and in Spain they are called cigarra.

EATING LOBSTER

All types of lobster are best cooked simply to allow the delicate flavour to speak for itself. They can be boiled in salted water or court-bouillon and served hot with melted butter or cold with mayonnaise, grilled (broiled) or fried in the shell with oil and butter. A plain lobster can be the crowning glory of a seafood platter.

Classical French cookery has a plethora of rich lobster recipes that reflect the luxurious quality of these crustaceans. These dishes include Lobster with Wholegrain Mustard and Cream (page 98), Seafood in Puff Pastry (page 120), and the world-famous Lobster Thermidor (page 96), with its brandy and mustard-flavoured sauce.

More contemporary recipes combine lobster with Asian flavours

Left: The Balmain bug is a warm-water variety of squat lobster from Australia that has sweet flesh.

such as ginger and chillies, but these spices should be used carefully and in moderation.

Lobster is superb with fresh pasta, and this is an excellent way to make a little meat go further. Use it as a filling for ravioli or toss it into tagliolini with lemon juice and butter. Cold boiled lobster can be diced and made into a lobster cocktail or added to a salad. When cooking lobster, use the shells to use in a stock or soup.

The increased availability in lobster has led to a rise in popularity in snacks, lunch and salad dishes. Steamed tails are a quick and easy way to obtain sweet lobster meat and ideal for making the ever-popular New England-style lobster rolls. Combined with creamy Greek yogurt and a dash of lemon or lime, lobster makes a delicious filling for wraps or baguettes. It's great tossed with warm new potatoes or pasta and your favourite salad ingredients and a tangy dressing for a quick lunch, or for a simple turf and surf burger, mix cooked lobster meat with mayo to top a beefburger.

CRABS

There are dozens of varieties of crab, ranging from hefty common crabs to tiny shore crabs that are good only for making soup. They are great wanderers, travelling hundreds of miles in a year from feeding to spawning grounds. As a result, crabs are often caught in baited pots sited on the sea bed far from the shore. As their bodies mature, crabs become too big for their shells and shed them while they grow a new carapace. At first the new shells are soft. These 'soft-shell' crabs are a delicacy and can be eaten shell and all. Female crabs, known as hens, have sweeter flesh than the males, but are smaller and their claws contain less flesh. In France, crab is called crabe, tourteau (common edible crab) or araignée (spider crab). In Italy, it is called granchio or granseola; and in Spain, cangrejo or centolla.

BLUE CRAB
(Callinectes sapidus)
These crabs have steely-grey bodies and very bright, almost electric blue legs and claws. They are found in

Above: Soft-shell crabs.

American waters and are prized for their very white meat.

Soft-shell crabs are blue crabs that have shed their hard carapaces, leaving them beautifully tender, with sweet creamy flesh. They are extremely delicate and do not keep or travel well, so they are generally sold frozen, although you may find fresh soft-shell crabs in the United States in the summer months.

COMMON EDIBLE CRAB/BROWN CRAB
(Cancer pagarus)
The bodies of these large brownish-red crabs can measure well over

Above: Common or brown crab.

20cm/8in. They have big, powerful claws that can deliver an extremely nasty nip, but they contain plenty of tasty meat. Common edible crabs are found on Atlantic coasts and parts of the Mediterranean.

These are the perfect crabs for boiling to serve simply cold with mayonnaise for an appetizing starter. After cooking, the rich, meaty claws can be removed from the shell in one piece, marinated in a dressing and served as a cocktail snack. The claw meat is also often served deep-fried. The liver and roe of these crabs are also delicious.

DUNGENESS/CALIFORNIA CRAB
(Cancer magister)
These trapezium-shaped crabs are found all along the Pacific coast, from Mexico to Alaska. They are very similar to common edible crabs and can be cooked in the same way.

KING CRAB (Paralithodes camtschiatica)
Looking like gigantic spiny spiders, king crabs are hideous to behold, but very good to eat. Their very size is awe-inspiring; a mature male king crab can weigh up to 12kg/26½lb and measure 1m/3ft across. Their triangular bodies are bright red, with a pale creamy underside. Every part

Below: Blue crabs.

tastes good, from the body meat to that from the narrow claws and long, dangly legs.

Only male king crabs are sold; they are much larger and meatier than the females. Cooked legs are available frozen, and king crab meat is frequently canned. Unlike most crab meat, canned king crab is of excellent quality and highly prized. The best canned crab meat comes from Alaska, Japan and Russia, where it is sold as Kamchatka crab.

SNOW CRAB (Chionoetes spp)
Also known as queen crabs, these crabs from the north Pacific have roundish pinkish-brown bodies and exceptionally long legs. The delicious, sweet flesh is difficult to remove from the body, but the claw meat is more accessible. Snow crab meat is usually sold frozen or canned.

SPIDER CRAB (Maia squinado)
These alarming-looking crabs have spiny shells and long slender legs, which give them the appearance of enormous reddish-pink spiders; hence their alternative name of 'sea spider'. Those found along the Atlantic coasts measure about 20cm/8in across, but the giant species, found in the waters around Japan, measures up to 40cm/16in, with a huge claw span of almost 3m/9¾ft.

STONE CRAB (family Lithodidae)
Similar in appearance to king crabs, stone crabs live at great depths. They do have a superb flavour, but are usually sold frozen or canned rather than fresh.

SWIMMING CRAB (family Portunidae)
The main distinguishing feature of these crabs is their extra pair of legs, shaped rather like paddles. Among the many species of swimming crabs are mud or mangrove, shore and velvet crabs. Shore crabs are eaten in Italy in their soft-shelled state; they also make delicious soup. Mud crabs, which have excellent claw meat, are particularly popular in Australia and South-east Asia.

EATING CRAB
Crab can be cooked in a multitude of ways. The sweet, succulent meat is rich and filling, so needs a light touch when cooking; refreshing flavours suit it better than creamy sauces. Picking it out of the shell is fiddly, but the result is well worth the effort. Recipes for crab meat include devilled crab (where the meat is removed from the shell and cooked with mustard, horseradish, spices and breadcrumbs); crab mornay, in which the meat is combined with a Gruyère cheese sauce enriched with sherry and mushrooms, and potted crab.

The flesh marries well with clean Asian flavours such as lime juice, coriander (cilantro) and chilli; combined with these, it makes a delightful summer salad. Crab meat is perfect for fish cakes such as Maryland or Thai crab cakes. It also makes excellent soup; a classic Scottish dish is partan bree, a creamy crab soup made with fish stock, milk and rice.

In the shell, crab can be boiled and served with mayonnaise, steamed with aromatics or baked with ginger, chilli, garlic and spring onions (scallions).

Soft-shell crabs are usually lightly coated in flour and deep-fried. A Venetian speciality is molecchie fritte; the crabs are soaked in beaten egg before being fried. In China, soft-shell crabs are steamed, and served with a garnish of chilli or ginger. They can also be sautéed in butter and sprinkled with toasted almonds, or brushed with melted butter and lemon juice, then tossed lightly in flour before grilling or broiling.

Below: Swimming crabs.

PRAWNS AND SHRIMP

Thousands of species of prawns and shrimp are found in all of the world's oceans (in both warm water and cold water) and also in fresh water. In the UK fish trade, smaller prawns are known as shrimp, but in America, all sizes are known as shrimp.

COMMON PRAWN
(Palaemon serratus)
These translucent, brownish prawns can grow up to 10cm/4in in length. They are found in deep waters in the Atlantic Ocean and Mediterranean Sea, but related species are found throughout the world. They have an exceptionally good flavour and command high prices. They are also known as sword shrimp or Algerian shrimp.

In France, they are called crevette rose or bouquet; in Italy, they are gamberello; in Spain, camarón or quisquilla.

DEEP-SEA PRAWN (Pandalus borealis)
These cold-water prawns live at great depths in the North Sea. They have translucent pink bodies, which turn pale salmon-pink on cooking.

In France, these prawns are crevette; Italians know them as gambero; while in Spain they are called camarón.

Below: Deep sea prawns.

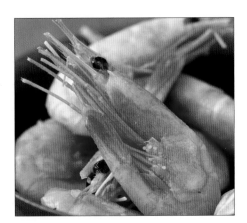

MEDITERRANEAN PRAWN
(Aristeus antennatus)
These large prawns can measure up to 10cm/4in. The colour varies but once cooked, they turn a brilliant red. The flesh is delicious and succulent. Usually sold cooked they should be served simply, with mayonnaise.

Mediterranean prawns are also known as blue or red shrimp. Called crevette rouge in France, they are called gambero rosso in Italy and carabinero in Spain.

COMMON/BROWN SHRIMP
(Crangon crangon)
These small shrimp have translucent grey bodies and measure only about 5cm/2in. When cooked, they turn brownish-grey. They are difficult to peel, but can be eaten whole and their flavour is incomparable. They are used to make potted shrimp.

The French call these shrimp crevette grise or boucaud; the Italians know them as gamberetto grigio; the Spanish quisquilla.

GULF PRAWNS/SHRIMP
(Hymenopenaeus robustus)
From the Gulf of Mexico, these are usually bright red. Gulf prawns can grow up to 40g/1½oz in weight, and have succulent flesh.

Below: Gulf shrimp.

Above: Jumbo prawns.

KURUMA/JAPANESE PRAWN
(Penaeus japonicus)
These large prawns are found in the Indo-Pacific region and the Red Sea, and can grow to 23cm/9in. They have yellowish tails flecked with black.

TIGER/KING PRAWN/JUMBO SHRIMP
(Penaeus monodon)
These huge prawns are found throughout the Indo-Pacific. They can grow up to 33cm/13in and are ideal for cooking on a barbecue. When raw, they are a translucent greenish-grey. Their flavour is not as good as that of cold-water prawns but they have succulent, firm flesh.

EATING PRAWNS
The cardinal rule is not to overcook them. Serve pre-cooked prawns with lemon and brown bread and butter, or in a prawn cocktail or salad. Small prawns or shrimp make an excellent filling for omelettes or tartlets.

Raw prawns can be boiled briefly in salt water or court-bouillon and are also delicious grilled or broiled whole in their shells, cooked on a barbecue, sautéed in garlic butter or deep-fried in batter; they are an essential ingredient of an Italian fritto misto. Raw, shelled prawns can also be used in stir-fries, fish pies and soups.

CRAYFISH AND LANGOUSTINES

There are two smaller members of the lobster family that are a popular choice worldwide. Crayfish are a freshwater species, whereas langoustines inhabit cold water oceans. Crayfish are also known as crawfish, crawdads, freshwater lobsters or mudbugs in different parts of the world. These tasty mini lobsters are usually a similar size and can be interchanged in recipes.

CRAYFISH (Astacus astacus)
AND YABBY (Cherax)

Crayfish are miniature freshwater lobsters, which grow to a maximum length of 10cm/4in. The exception is a species found in Tasmania, which can weigh up to 6kg/13lb. Crayfish have a superb flavour and, whatever their colour when alive, turn a glorious deep scarlet when cooked. Over 300 species are found throughout Europe, America and Australia. Britain's only native crayfish, the white claw, is under serious threat from the imported US signal crayfish, and is now a protected species.

In France, crayfish are called écrevisse; in Italy, gambero di fiume; in Spain, cangrejo de rio.

Fresh crayfish should be bought live. There is a lot of wastage, so

Below: Crayfish can come in a wide range of colours but all turn a deep scarlet colour when cooked.

Above: Crayfish are tiny freshwater lobsters; there are hundreds of species.

allow 8–12 crayfish per serving. Keep the shells to make stock to flavour soups and sauces. Frozen crayfish are better for made-up dishes than for eating on their own.

EATING CRAYFISH

Crayfish feature in many luxurious dishes, including bisque, sauces and mousses. They are superb poached in a court-bouillon for about 5 minutes and served cold with mayonnaise or hot with lemony melted butter. Only the tail and claw meat is eaten. The cleaned heads and shells can be used to make stock or soup.

LANGOUSTINES/DUBLIN BAY PRAWNS/SCAMPI/NORWAY LOBSTER
(Nephrops norvegicus)

Smaller relatives of lobsters, langoustines have smooth-shelled narrow bodies with long thin, knobbly claws. The largest can measure up to 23cm/9in, but the average length is about 12cm/4½in. Langoustines were originally found in Norway, hence their Latin name, and they are still sometimes known as Norway lobsters. Nowadays, they are caught all along the Atlantic coast, in the Adriatic and western Mediterranean where they are

particularly popular. The colder the water, the better the flavour.

The French know them as langoustine; the Italians call them scampo, while in Spain they are called cigala or langostina.

Langoustines deteriorate very rapidly once caught, so are often cooked and frozen at sea. If you find live langoustines, and can be certain of cooking them soon after purchase, they will be an excellent buy. It is important to check that they are still moving. Unlike other crustaceans, langoustines are naturally pink when raw and stay the same colour when cooked. They are also available frozen, often as scampi tails. If they have been shelled, allow about 115g/4oz per person; you will need twice this quantity if the langoustines are in the shell.

EATING LANGOUSTINES

Properly (very briefly) cooked, the flavour is exquisite. Roast in oil and garlic for 3–5 minutes; split and grill on a barbecue for 2 minutes each side; or poach in stock and serve hot with melted butter. The tails can be baked au gratin in a creamy sauce or, for a special treat, served Scottish-style in a whisky-flavoured sauce.

Below: Langoustines, which are also known as Dublin Bay prawns and scampi.

EQUIPMENT

Although it is perfectly possible to prepare and cook lobster without special equipment, there are a few items which make the process much easier. Some, such as large pots and pans and sharp knives, are probably already a part of your kitchen, but others, like a pick and crackers, might need to be bought so that you can make the most of your lobster.

CHEF'S KNIFE
A large heavy knife with a 20–25cm/8–10in blade is essential for splitting open lobster, crawfish, crabs and other large crustaceans.

FILLETING KNIFE
A sharp knife with a flexible blade, which is at least 15cm/6in long, this is useful for opening a variety of shellfish and should be razor-sharp.

PARING KNIFE
This is a small knife with a straight, sharp blade 7.5–13cm/3–5in long. Its thin, narrow blade tapers to a point at the tip. It is easy to handle and is very useful for deveining and butterflying prawns as well as for peeling and chopping a whole range of small ingredients such as garlic, herbs and vegetables.

CLEAVER
This wide-bladed, heavy knife is a good alternative to a chef's knife for splitting lobster. Often used in Asian cookery, it can also be used for finely chopping ingredients.

SCISSORS OR POULTRY SHEARS
A sturdy pair of scissors or poultry shears are particularly useful for cutting through the top and bottom shell of a cooked lobster and also for preparing prawns and crayfish. It is also possible to buy lobster shears – specifically designed to cut through the shell. But unless lobster is going to be a regular dish, scissors or poultry shears will do the job well, are more versatile and less expensive.

LOBSTER PICK
Choose a pick with a two-pronged fork at the end to allow quick and easy removal of the flesh from lobster and crab legs.

LOBSTER CRACKERS
Specialist lobster crackers are like hinged nutcrackers (sometimes made in the shape of lobster claws) with ridges on the inside to give a good grip. They make easy work of cracking the shells of lobster, crab and other hard-shelled seafood.

POTS AND PANS
A selection of large, deep pans, oven trays and steamers are useful for cooking shellfish. Steamers are a good buy as steaming keeps the flesh of fish and shellfish tender. A stainless steel steamer is a good choice for cooking shellfish, fish and vegetables. Buy a universal steamer to fit on existing pans or purchase a stacking set of two perforated steamers plus a solid base-pan – known as a three-tier steamer. For a more economical option choose a Chinese bamboo steamer. As they come in a variety of sizes, choose one to go over pans already in your kitchen. Bamboo or stainless steel steamers can be stacked one on top of each other so several layers of food can be cooked at one time.

Above: Using the right tools will help you extract every tender morsel from your prized lobster.

Left: Use a chef's knife to split open the hard shells of large crustaceans.

Right: A lobster pick makes it easier to extract meat from inside the shell.

Above: A large, deep pan for preparing lobster stock should have handles on the side for ease of lifting.

STOCK POT
This is a large, deep pan for making stock and for cooking whole lobster. Heavy duty stainless steel will last for many years. Choose a pan with handles on the side – this makes it easier to lift when it is full.

ROASTING TIN
Essential for grilling, broiling or baking parboiled lobster, the tin needs to be large enough to hold two halves of a split lobster. The roasting tin should also be strong enough to withstand direct heat and should not rust. Heavy stainless steel or enamel roasting tins are by far the best choices.

COOK'S WOODEN MALLET
This is useful to crack open the claws and shell of lobster and other shellfish. Alternatively a wooden rolling pin can be used.

Right: Sturdy metal tongs will make handling cooked lobster much easier.

METAL SKEWER
A strong metal skewer can be used as an alternative to a lobster pick to extract the meat out of lobster and crab shells. It can also be used to kill a live lobster that has been rendered unconscious by chilling. Push the skewer straight through the centre of the cross on its head to kill it instantly.

WOODEN SKEWERS
These are suitable for kebabs that are to be grilled or barbecued. Soak the skewers in cold water for 20 minutes, before threading any ingredients on, to prevent them from burning.

BARBECUE RACK
For cooking whole prawns, lobster or crayfish or kebabs over charcoal. To prevent food from sticking, oil the rack before cooking.

FINE METAL SIEVE
An essential piece of equipment to make smooth stock and soups. The finer the sieve the better as the finished result will be smoother.

Above: A large, sturdy barbecue rack will enable you to cook complete lobster easily.

TONGS
A sturdy pair of long metal tongs is very useful for removing whole, cooked lobster from a pan of boiling water. Shorter tongs – metal or wooden – can be used for turning smaller shellfish such as prawns when pan-frying or barbecuing.

BUYING, PREPARING AND COOKING LARGE SHELLFISH

The term 'shellfish' is loosely applied to any seafood other than fish. Strictly speaking, it means aquatic invertebrates with shells or shell-like carapaces. This includes the crustaceans – lobsters, crabs, prawns, shrimp and similar creatures – as well as some molluscs, such as clams, mussels and oysters. For convenience, however, the category extends to other molluscs too, such as the cephalopods (octopus, squid and cuttlefish) and lesser-known sea creatures, such as sea urchins.

When discussing large shellfish, or crustaceans, it is impossible to divorce preparation and cooking techniques, since one is bound up so closely with the other. Lobsters, crabs and crayfish are cooked live, whereas prawns, shrimp and langoustines are not.

Although crustaceans need very little cooking to enhance their already superb flavour, all types must be cooked. Unlike fish, the larger specimens can be boiled. Many of the methods used for cooking fish are also suitable for shellfish – poaching, frying, grilling, broiling and steaming.

BUYING LOBSTER AND CRAB

Live lobsters or crabs should smell very fresh and still be lively and aggressive when picked up. The tails of lobsters should spring back sharply when they are opened out. Crabs should feel heavy for their size, but you should make sure this is not because there is water inside the shell. Shake them – any sloshing sounds are a bad sign. The shell

Above: European lobster meat is highly prized.

should neither be soft nor should it contain any cracks or holes.

It is a good idea to check that lobsters and crabs have both claws, as one may often be lost in a fight. Similarly, look to see that the lobster's antennae are long: in captivity lobsters tend to eat each other's antennae so short ones suggest the lobster has been in a tank a long time.

Always buy fresh cooked lobsters or crabs from a reputable supplier who cooks them fresh every day. The colour should be vibrant and the crustaceans ought to feel heavy for their size. Cooked lobsters should have their tails tightly curled under their bodies; avoid specimens with floppy tails, which may have been dead when they were cooked.

You can buy frozen raw lobsters, which have the advantage of having already been killed. These should be defrosted before cooking. Frozen ready-cooked whole lobsters have become much more widely available in recent years and are the simplest of all to use. Allow to thaw completely

Left: Live lobsters should be lively.

Above: Try to keep live lobsters submerged in ice.

in the refrigerator overnight, and then remove the meat, as described on page 20 (unless cooking and serving in the shell). When calculating how much you should buy, allow about 450g/1lb total weight (including the shell) per person.

STORING

For practical reasons you will wish to cook live lobsters or crabs on the day you buy them. In addition, live

Below: Freeze the lobster for 2 hours to render it unconscious and then despatch it with a sharp knife.

lobsters start to deteriorate as soon as they are out of seawater so it is best to cook them immediately.

Cooked lobster can be refrigerated but only for 1–2 days.

PREPARING AND COOKING LOBSTER

The most humane way to kill a live lobster is to render it unconscious by placing it in a tray and covering it with crushed ice for 2 hours. Alternatively, put the lobster in the freezer for 2 hours. When the lobster is no longer moving, place it on a chopping board and drive the tip of a sharp heavy knife or strong skewer through the centre of the cross on its head. Death is instantaneous.

If you can't face stabbing the lobster, put it in a large pan of cold, heavily salted water and bring slowly to the boil. The lobster will expire before the water boils.

Alternatively, you can add the comatose lobster to a large pan of boiling water. Plunge it in, head first, and immediately clamp on the lid. Bring the water back to the boil.

Below: You can also drop the frozen lobster straight into salted boiling water, without stabbing first.

Above: Don't cook more than two lobsters at a time.

Lower the heat and simmer the lobster gently for about 15 minutes for the first 450g/1lb and then allow 10 minutes more for each subsequent 450g/1lb, up to a maximum of 40 minutes. When cooked, the lobster will turn a deep brick-red. Drain and leave to cool, if not eating hot.

If cooking two or more lobsters in the same pan, wait until the water comes back to the boil before adding the second one.

Below: Lobster is cooked as soon as it turns bright red all over.

REMOVING THE MEAT FROM A COOKED LOBSTER

1 Lay the lobster on its back and twist off the large legs and claws.

2 Crack open the claws with a wooden mallet or the back of a heavy knife and remove the meat, keeping the pieces as large as possible. Scoop out the leg meat with a lobster pick or the handle of a small teaspoon.

TOMALLEY AND CORAL
Keep the greenish tomalley (liver) and the coral (roe), which are delicious. The roe is only found in the female lobsters. Both are usually added to a sauce, as they have quite a strong, almost pungent flavour, although some people like to eat them as they are. The creamy flesh close to the shell can also be scraped out and used in a sauce.

3 On a chopping board, stretch out the body of the lobster so that its tail is extended.

4 Turn it on to its back and, holding it firmly with one hand, use a sharp, heavy knife to cut the lobster neatly in half along its entire length.

5 Discard the whitish sac and the feathery gills from the head and the grey-black intestinal thread that runs down the tail.

6 Carefully remove all the meat from each half of the tail – it should come out in one piece.

COOK'S TIP Removing the meat from a whole lobster can be fiddly and time-consuming but the advantage is that you can use the pieces of shell, once all the meat has been removed, to make lobster stock, see opposite.

GRILLING LOBSTER

Place the live lobster in the freezer for 2 hours to render it unconscious then plunge it head first into boiling water. Boil the lobster for 3 minutes only, drain, split in half and clean.

Preheat the grill or broiler to high. Lay the halves of the lobster cut side up in a grill pan, brush generously with melted butter and cook for about 10 minutes, spooning on more melted butter halfway through.

BARBECUEING LOBSTER

Prepare the lobster as for grilling. Brush the cut sides with butter seasoned with garlic or cayenne and fresh herbs. Grill, cut side down, over moderately hot coals for about 5 minutes, then turn the halves over and grill them on the shell for 5 minutes more. Turn the lobster halves over once more, brush the flesh with more melted butter and grill it, flesh side down, for 3–4 minutes more.

EATING A WHOLE LOBSTER

Eating a whole lobster might seem daunting, and certainly takes a while, but follow these steps to ensure success. You can either eat as you shell, or shell it all first.

1 First remove the claws, then separate the tail and legs from the body. Pull the top shell away from the body and discard. Inside the cavity you will see the tomally; remove it together with the roe if there is any. Then take out the meat in one piece and set aside or eat it.

2 Next suck the meat out of each of the legs, or prize it out with a skewer or lobster pick.

3 Now go back to the claws and use lobster crackers to crunch them so they split and the meat can be removed. Be careful not to use too much force or you will splinter the shell and spoil the meat.

4 Finally work on the tail: first pick off the tail flaps and suck the meat out of the holes. Next extract the tail meat out of the shell in one piece by poking your finger in the base of the tail at the smallest opening.

LOBSTER STOCK

If you've bought a fresh or frozen cooked whole lobster, the best way to make the most of it is to use the shell, once you've extracted the meat, to make a delicious stock. From soups and casseroles to risottos and sauces, a good-quality home-made stock can really make the difference to the flavour of your meal.

MAKES 2 LITRES/3½ PINTS
1 whole cooked lobster shell (meat removed)
2 lemon slices
2 peppercorns
1 bay leaf
4 sprigs fresh flat leaf parsley
1 small onion, halved

1 Place the lobster shell, together with all the pieces of leg, claw and shell in a large, deep-sided heavy pan. Add the lemon slices, peppercorns, bay leaf, parsley and onion, and cover with 2 litres/3½ pints/8 cups of cold water.

2 On a high heat bring the water to the boil and then cover and reduce the heat to low. Allow the stock to simmer gently for 1½–2 hours. Give the lobster pieces a stir occasionally to avoid anything sticking on the bottom of the pan.

3 Remove the pan from the heat and pour the stock through a large metal colander. You might need to strain it again through a finer sieve or strainer to catch all the pieces of shell. Set aside to cool and then chill in the refrigerator. Use within 2 days or freeze for up to 1 month.

PREPARING AND COOKING CRAB

Submerge the live crab in ice, or leave it in the freezer for 2–3 hours until it is comatose, then lay it on its back on a chopping board, lift up the tail flap and look for a small hole at the base of a distinct groove. Drive a sturdy skewer into this hole, then carefully push the skewer between the mouth plates between the eyes. The crab is now ready for cooking.

Alternatively, cook the crab directly from the freezer. Plunge the chilled or dead crab into a pan of salted, boiling water, bring back to the boil and cook for 10–12 minutes; or place it in a pan of cold, salted water and bring it slowly to the boil. The latter is thought to be more humane, as the crab becomes sleepy and expires before the water is at boiling point. Whichever way you choose, calculate the cooking time from the moment that the water boils.

REMOVING THE MEAT FROM A COOKED CRAB

1 Lay the cooked crab on its back on a large chopping board.

2 Hold the crab firmly with one hand and break off the tail flap. Twist off both the claws and the legs.

3 Stand it on its head and insert a heavy knife between the body and shell. Twist the knife firmly to separate them so that you can lift the honeycomb body out.

4 Alternatively, hold the crab firmly and use your thumbs to push down and ease the body out of the shell.

5 Remove and discard the feathery, grey gills (these are unattractively but descriptively known as 'dead men's fingers'), which are attached to either side of the body.

6 Press down on the top shell to detach the spongy stomach sac – this is found directly behind the mouth. Cut the honeycomb body into quarters with a large, heavy knife.

7 Carefully pick out the white meat, using a skewer. Place this in a small bowl, keeping it separate from the brown meat.

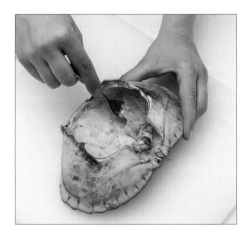

8 Use a teaspoon to scoop out the brown meat from the back shell, transferring it to another bowl. Then scoop out the thin solid brown meat from inside the flaps.

9 Crack open the claws and legs with a mallet (or use the back of a heavy knife), then remove the claw meat in the largest possible pieces. Pick or scrape out the leg meat with a lobster pick or a skewer.

PREPARING AND COOKING PRAWNS, SHRIMP, AND CRAYFISH

There is some confusion over the terms prawn and shrimp. In America, the word shrimp refers to all sizes and types of prawns, but in most countries shrimps are a tiny separate species. Prawns and shrimp are not sold alive, but crayfish must be as their flesh deteriorates quickly after death and can become poisonous. If you buy frozen prawns or shrimp get them into your freezer as soon as possible. Do not buy prawns or shrimp that have been frozen and then thawed.

If you buy them with the shells on, allow about 300g/11oz prawns or shrimp per serving. Some crustaceans – Dublin Bay prawns, for example – tend to be sold shelled, without the heads. If you buy these in the shell, remember that there will be a lot of wastage (up to 80 per cent) so buy a generous amount.

Fresh prawns and shrimp should be eaten as soon as possible after purchase. Crayfish, including the yabby, however, are none too fussy about what they eat, so need to be purged after purchase. Place them in a bowl, cover with a damp dish towel and leave in the coldest part of the refrigerator for 24 hours.

Above: Crayfish should be bought while still alive and purged before cooking.

PEELING AND DEVEINING RAW PRAWNS

Raw prawns and large shrimp are usually peeled before they are cooked. For the best results, raw prawns must have their intestinal tracts removed before cooking, a relatively simple process that is known as 'deveining'. It is not necessary to devein very small shrimp.

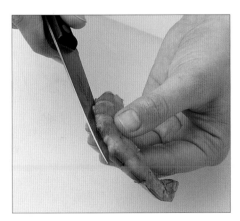

1 Pull off the head and legs from each prawn or shrimp, then carefully peel off the body shell with your fingers. Leave on the tail 'fan' if you like.

2 To remove the intestinal vein from prawns, make a shallow incision down the centre of the curved back of the prawn using a small sharp knife, cutting all the way from the tail to the head.

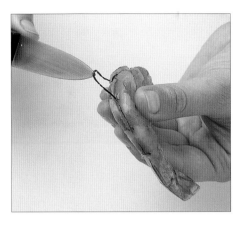

3 Pick out the thin black vein that runs the length of the prawn with the tip of the knife and discard.

POACHING PRAWNS

The sweet, meaty flavour of prawns make them an ideal choice for poaching. Raw prawns are best poached in sea water. Failing that, add a well-flavoured fish stock or salted water to a large saucepan.

Add the shelled and deveined, raw prawns and gently heat the liquid. Cook on a low heat until the prawns have changed colour and are just opaque. This should take no more than 3 minutes. Take care not to overcook the prawns as they will become rubbery.

Above: All fresh, raw prawns and shrimp should have crisp, firm shells and a clean smell.

GRILLING LARGE PRAWNS ON THE BARBECUE

1 Preheat the grill, broiler or barbecue to hot. Butterfly the shellfish by laying them on their backs and splitting them in half lengthways, without cutting right through to the back shell.

2 Open the shellfish out like a book and brush the cut sides all over with a mixture of olive oil and lemon juice.

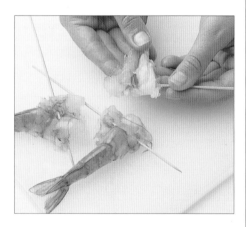

3 Thread the butterflied shellfish on to skewers or lay them in a grill or broiler pan or on a barbecue rack. Cook for 2–3 minutes on each side. If the shellfish is already cooked, place on the barbecue for about half this time. Any longer and the meat will become dry and rubbery.

SHELLING COOKED PRAWNS, AND LANGOUSTINES

1 Twist off the heads and, in the case of langoustines, the claws.

2 Squeeze the shellfish along their length and pull off the shell and the legs with your fingers.

3 To keep the tail fan, peel off the last piece of body shell, or, squeeze the end of the tail and remove.

FANTAIL PRAWNS

This way of serving large prawns comes from China. The cooked prawns, with their bright red tails, are supposed to resemble the legendary phoenix, which in China is a symbol of dignity and good luck.

1 Remove the heads from the prawns and peel away most of the body shell with your fingers. Leave a little of the shell to keep the tail 'fan' intact.

2 Make a long shallow incision in the back of each prawn and remove the black intestinal vein with the point of the knife.

3 Hold the prepared prawns by the tails and dip them lightly in a little seasoned cornflour/cornstarch, and then in a frothy batter before deep-frying them in hot oil until the tails, which are free from batter, turn red.

SHELLING COOKED CRAYFISH

1 Hold the cooked, cooled crayfish between your finger and thumb and gently twist off the tail.

2 Hold the tail shell between your thumb and index finger, twist and pull off the flat end; the thread-like intestinal tract will come away, discard this. Peel the tail.

3 Hold the head and thorax in one hand. Use the other finger to prise off the whole underside, including the gills and innards, and discard these. Finally, gently twist off the claws from the head.

POTTED SHRIMP

These are very simple to make and will keep for several days. If possible, use fresh, not frozen, small brown shrimp. They are tedious to peel, but well worth the effort. Serve with brown bread or toast and lemon wedges.

SERVES 4
350g/12oz/1½ cups butter
225g/8oz cooked peeled shrimp, thawed if frozen
1 bay leaf
1 large blade of mace or 2.5ml/½ tsp ground mace
ground black pepper and cayenne pepper

1 Melt 250g/9oz/generous 1 cup of the butter in a pan. Add the shrimp, bay leaf, mace and seasoning. Heat gently, then discard the bay leaf and mace.

2 Divide the shrimp equally between four ramekins, leaving enough space at the top for a layer of butter, and leave to set.

3 Clarify the remaining butter, by placing it in a small pan and heating very gently over a low heat until melted and foaming.

4 Strain the butter through a sieve lined with muslin or cheesecloth into a small bowl, leaving the milky solids at the base of the pan.

5 Spoon the clarified butter over the potted shrimp, making sure they are completely covered. When cool, transfer the ramekins to the refrigerator and chill. Potted shrimp can be kept in the refrigerator for up to 2–3 days.

6 To serve, toast thin slices of good white bread and spread the potted shrimp over while the toast is hot, so that the butter melts slightly.

SAUCES FOR SHELLFISH

Many types of shellfish are so deliciously rich that they do not need to be cooked in a sauce, but a good accompanying sauce will certainly enhance plainly boiled, grilled or barbecued lobster, prawns or crab.

NEVER-FAIL MAYONNAISE

Classic mayonnaise has a reputation for being difficult to make, but this simple version takes away the mystique. The essential thing is to have all the ingredients at room temperature before you begin.

SERVES 4–6
1 egg, plus 1 egg yolk
5ml/1 tsp Dijon mustard
juice of 1 large lemon
175ml/6fl oz/¾ cup olive oil
175ml/6fl oz/¾ cup grapeseed, sunflower or corn oil
salt and ground white pepper

1 Put the whole egg and yolk in a food processor and process for 20 seconds. Add the mustard, half the lemon juice and a generous pinch of salt and pepper. Process for about 30 seconds, until thoroughly mixed.

2 With the motor running, slowly pour in the oils through the feeder tube in a thin, steady stream. Process until the oils are incorporated and the mayonnaise is pale and thick. Taste and add more lemon juice and seasoning, if necessary.

BEURRE BLANC

This light sauce goes perfectly with poached or grilled shellfish.

SERVES 4
3 shallots, very finely chopped
45ml/3 tbsp dry white wine or court-bouillon
45ml/3 tbsp white wine or tarragon vinegar
115g/4oz/½ cup chilled unsalted butter, diced
lemon juice (optional)
salt and ground white pepper

1 Put the shallots in a small pan with the wine or court-bouillon and vinegar. Bring to the boil and cook over a high heat until only about 30ml/2 tbsp liquid remains. Remove the pan from the heat and leave to cool until just lukewarm.

2 Whisk in the chilled butter, a piece at a time, to make a creamy sauce. Make sure each piece is incorporated before adding the next. Season with salt and pepper and add a little lemon juice to taste, if you like. Serve immediately, or keep warm in a double boiler over simmering water.

HOLLANDAISE SAUCE

This rich sauce goes well with any poached shellfish. It is served warm. As the egg yolks are barely cooked, it is best not to serve to children, the elderly or invalids.

SERVES 4
115g/4oz/½ cup unsalted butter
2 egg yolks
15–30ml/1–2 tbsp lemon juice or white wine or tarragon vinegar
salt and ground white pepper

1 Melt the butter in a small pan. Whisk the egg yolks, lemon juice or vinegar and salt and pepper in a large heatproof bowl. Place the bowl on a pan of simmering water.

2 Slowly add the melted butter, first a spoonful at a time, and then in a steady stream, into the egg yolk mixture, beating vigorously with a wooden spoon constantly to make a smooth, creamy sauce.

3 If the sauce starts to split or separate, add an ice cube and beat vigorously. Serve warm.

BUTTER AND HERB SAUCE

You can use just one favourite herb or several for this recipe. The light and fragrant sauce can be served as a dip or to pour over poached fish or shellfish. For a hint of spice and extra colour add a little cayenne pepper.

SERVES 4
2 good handfuls mixed fresh herbs, plus extra herb leaves to garnish
115g/4oz/½ cup butter
pinch of cayenne pepper (optional)
salt and ground black pepper

1 Chop the herbs coarsely or finely, as you prefer.

2 Melt the butter in a small pan. As soon as the butter sizzles, remove from the heat and sprinkle in the herbs, the cayenne pepper (if using) with salt and pepper to taste. Stir well.

3 Serve, garnished with extra herbs.

CRAYFISH SAUCE

This sauce, also known as Nantua sauce, is perfect for using up the shells left over from seafood recipes. It can also be made with other crustaceans, such as lobster or large prawns. Use it to enhance any white fish or shellfish.

SERVES 4
1 cooked crayfish, or about 450g/1lb other crustaceans
40g/1½ oz/3 tbsp butter
15ml/1 tbsp olive oil
45ml/3 tbsp brandy
500ml/17fl oz/generous 2 cups fish or shellfish stock
15ml/1 tbsp plain/all-purpose flour
45ml/3 tbsp double/heavy cream
2 egg yolks
salt and ground white pepper

1 Remove the tail meat from the crayfish and keep for another recipe. Using a meat cleaver or wooden mallet break up the shells and legs and crush them coarsely in a food processor.

2 Melt 25g/1oz/2 tbsp of the butter with the oil in a heavy-based pan, add the shells and cook for about 3

minutes, stirring frequently, until the crayfish has turned bright red.

3 Add the brandy and fish or shellfish stock, bring to the boil, then simmer for 10 minutes.

4 Mash the remaining butter with the flour to make beurre manié, or a paste. Gradually whisk this into the sauce, a small piece at a time, and cook gently until thickened.

5 Season the sauce with salt and white pepper and strain it through a fine sieve or strainer. Return the sauce to a clean pan and stir in the cream on a low heat to bring it back to just below boiling point.

6 Beat the egg yolks lightly in a bowl and mix in a couple of spoonfuls of the hot sauce.

7 Return the mixture to the pan and cook gently until smooth. Adjust the seasoning and serve warm with fish or seafood.

Left: Crayfish pots stacked up ready for the next fishing trip.

FIERY CITRUS SALSA

This unusual salsa makes a fantastic marinade for shellfish, and it is especially delicious drizzled over barbecued lobster.

SERVES 4
1 orange, peeled
1 green apple, peeled
2 fresh red chillies, halved and seeded
1 garlic clove
8 fresh mint leaves
juice of 1 lemon
salt and ground black pepper

1 Divide the orange into segments, and slice the apple into wedges and remove the core.

2 Place the chillies in a blender or food processor with the orange segments, apple wedges, garlic and fresh mint. Process for a few seconds until smooth. Then, with the motor running, slowly pour the lemon juice into the mixture.

3 Season to taste with a little salt and black pepper. Pour into a bowl and serve immediately.

GREEN TARTARE SAUCE

A herby version of the traditional tartare sauce that's good with all kinds of shellfish.

SERVES 4
120ml/4fl oz/½ cup crème fraîche or Greek yogurt
10ml/2 tsp wholegrain mustard
2 garlic cloves, crushed
30–45ml/2–3 tbsp fresh lime juice
60ml/4 tbsp chopped fresh parsley
30ml/2 tbsp snipped chives
salt and ground black pepper

1 Blend the crème fraîche or yogurt, mustard, garlic, lime juice, parsley, chives and seasoning together in a food processor or blender.

2 Transfer into a small bowl to serve. You can make this sauce in advance and store in the refrigerator for up to 2 days.

LEMON AND LIME SAUCE

This is a tangy, refreshing sauce that will perfectly complement rich shellfish dishes.

SERVES 4
1 lemon
2 limes
50g/2oz/¼ cup caster/superfine sugar
25ml/1½ tbsp arrowroot

1 Using a citrus zester, peel the rinds thinly from the lemon and limes taking care not to cut into the pith. Squeeze the juice from the fruit. Place the rind in a pan, cover with water and bring to the boil. Drain through a sieve or strainer and reserve the rind.

2 In a bowl, mix a little sugar with the arrowroot. Blend in 30–45ml/2–3 tbsp water to give a smooth paste.

3 Heat 300ml/½ pint/1¼ cups water in a saucepan, pour in the arrowroot mixture, and stir constantly until the sauce boils and thickens. Stir in the remaining sugar, citrus juice and reserved rind. Keep the sauce hot until you are ready to serve.

STEAMED LOBSTER TAILS

Lobster tails are quick to prepare and cook and make an easy alternative to buying a whole lobster. Steaming them ensures they remain succulent and tasty and the cooking liquid can be reserved to use as stock for soup or risotto.

SERVES 4, AS A STARTER
2 lemon slices
bunch of fresh parsley
4 raw lobster tails, shell on

1 Pour 2.5cm/1in water into a medium pan and add the lemon and parsley. Bring to the boil.

2 Add the lobster tails, shell side down. Reduce the heat, cover and simmer gently for 8–10 minutes. The lobster should be firm and the shells a dark red colour.

3 Using a slotted spoon, remove the tails from the pan and reserve the cooking stock.

4 Place the tails, shell side down, on a plate and using sharp kitchen scissors or poultry shears cut through the underside of the body and gently pull the shell away.

Cook's Tip The tails can be bought fresh or, more normally, flash frozen. Always defrost thoroughly before cooking. Lobster tails make a delicious main or starter drizzled with any of the sauces in this section. Or serve simply with melted butter and a little lemon or lime juice.

Right: The tails can be served hot or cold and whole or chopped. Serve with a sauce or use in your chosen recipe.

5 Using a sharp knife remove the dark black thread that runs along the length of the tail.

6 Strain the reserved stock and allow it to cool to room temperature, then chill in the refrigerator for up to 2 days or freeze for up to 1 month.

SOUPS AND BISQUES

These steaming bowls of deeply-flavoured
seafood broth are probably the best ways to make
the most of lobster and crabs, as the stock has such
an amazing taste. This chapter includes flavours
from around the world.

LOBSTER BISQUE

SERVES 6

500g/1¼lb cooked lobster in its shell
75g/3oz/6 tbsp unsalted butter
1 onion, chopped
1 carrot, diced
1 celery stick, diced
45ml/3 tbsp brandy, plus extra for
serving
250ml/8fl oz/1 cup dry white wine
1 litre/1¾ pints/4 cups fish stock
15ml/1 tbsp tomato purée/paste
75g/3oz/scant ½ cup long grain rice
1 fresh bouquet garni
150ml/ ¼ pint/ ⅔ cup double/heavy
cream, plus extra to garnish
salt, ground white pepper and cayenne
pepper

Bisque is a luxurious, smooth and velvety soup of French origin. The whole lobster is used, even the shell, which makes a sumptuous broth flavoured with wine and brandy.

1 Cut the lobster into chunky pieces. Melt half the butter in a large pan, add the vegetables and cook over a low heat until soft. Add the lobster and stir well. Pour over the brandy and set it alight.

2 When the flames die down, add the wine and boil until reduced by half. Pour in the fish stock and simmer for 2–3 minutes. Remove the lobster. Stir in the tomato purée and rice, add the bouquet garni and cook for approximately 15 minutes, until the rice is tender. Remove the lobster meat from the shell and return the shell pieces to the pan. Dice the lobster meat and set it aside.

3 When the rice is cooked, remove the pieces of shell. Tip the mixture into a blender or food processor and process until smooth. Press through a fine strainer placed over a clean pan. Stir, then heat until almost boiling. Season with salt, pepper and cayenne, then lower the heat and stir in the cream.

4 Dice the remaining butter and whisk it into the bisque. Add the diced lobster meat and serve immediately. Pour a teaspoonful of brandy into each soup bowl, top with a spoonful of cream, and a sprinkle of cayenne.

Energy 406kcal/1684kJ; Protein 20.3g; Carbohydrate 13.7g, of which sugars 3.1g; Fat 25.2g, of which saturates 15g; Cholesterol 153mg; Calcium 84mg; Fibre 0.7g; Sodium 365mg.

CREAMY LOBSTER SOUP

SERVES 4

50g/2oz/¼ cup unsalted butter
50g/2oz/½ cup plain/all-purpose flour
700ml/1 pint 3½fl oz/scant 3 cups
  fish stock
5ml/1 tsp paprika
1 egg yolk
120ml/4fl oz/½ cup double/heavy
  cream
250g/9oz cooked lobster meat, chopped
  into bitesize pieces
15ml/1 tbsp lemon juice
sprigs of fresh dill, to garnish
salt and ground white pepper

Energy 348kcal/1444kJ; Protein 12.2g; Carbohydrate 10.9g, of
which sugars 0.8g; Fat 28.8g, of which saturates 17g;
Cholesterol 184mg; Calcium 65mg; Fibre 0.4g; Sodium 383mg.

The delicious and delicate sweet flavour of lobster meat gives a distinctive taste to this soup. Paprika and lemon juice contrast well with the lobster. The roux method used is unusual for a soup but it works well to give a smooth, creamy texture.

1 Melt the butter in a large heavy pan, stir in the flour to make a roux and cook gently over a low heat for 30 seconds, without colouring. Remove from the heat and gradually stir in the fish stock to form a smooth sauce.

2 Return the pan to the heat and, stirring all the time, cook until the sauce boils and thickens. Add the paprika and season to taste with salt and pepper.

3 In a small bowl, mix the egg yolk and cream together, then stir into the soup and heat gently, taking care not to let the mixture boil or the soup will curdle.

4 Add the lobster and lemon juice to the soup and heat gently. Pour the soup into individual serving bowls and serve hot, garnished with sprigs of dill.

LOBSTER, COCONUT AND CORIANDER SOUP

This recipe is based on the classic Brazilian seafood stew called Mocqueca. Quick and easy to prepare using ready-cooked lobster meat, the soup is packed with traditional Brazilian ingredients – creamy coconut milk, palm oil, fragrant fresh coriander and chilli to give it a spicy kick.

1 Heat the olive oil in a pan over a low heat. Stir in the onion and celery, and sauté gently for 5 minutes, until softened and translucent. Stir in the garlic and chilli and cook for a further 2 minutes.

2 Add the tomato and half the coriander and increase the heat. Cook, stirring, for 3 minutes, then add the stock. Bring to the boil, then simmer for 5 minutes.

3 Stir the lobster meat, coconut milk and palm oil into the pan and simmer over a very low heat for a further 5 minutes. The consistency should be thick, but not stew-like, so add some water if needed.

4 Stir in the lime juice and remaining coriander, then season with salt to taste. Serve in heated bowls with the chilli oil and lime wedges on the side.

VARIATION
The original Brazilian version of Mocqueca uses crab rather than lobster, so if you can't find lobster use the same amount of cooked crab meat instead.

SERVES 4
30ml/2 tbsp olive oil
1 onion, finely chopped
1 celery stick, finely chopped
2 garlic cloves, crushed
1 fresh red chilli, seeded and chopped
1 large tomato, peeled and chopped
45ml/3 tbsp chopped fresh coriander/
  cilantro
1 litre/1¾ pints/4 cups shellfish stock
500g/1¼lb cooked lobster meat
250ml/8fl oz/1 cup coconut milk
30ml/2 tbsp palm oil
juice of 1 lime
salt
hot chilli oil and lime wedges, to serve

Energy 228kcal/951kJ; Protein 23.6g; Carbohydrate 5.4g, of which sugars 5g; Fat 12.6g, of which saturates 3.7g; Cholesterol 90mg; Calcium 199mg; Fibre 1.1g; Sodium 767mg.

LOBSTER AND TOMATO SOUP

SERVES 4
800g/1¾lb cooked lobster in its shell
25g/1oz/2 tbsp unsalted butter
30ml/2 tbsp finely chopped shallot
2 red/bell peppers, seeded and chopped
2.5cm/1in fresh root ginger, finely
    chopped
1 clove garlic, finely chopped
60ml/4 tbsp brandy
30ml/2 tbsp tomato purée/paste
1.25 litres/2¼ pints/5½ cups water
15ml/1 tbsp sherry vinegar
15ml/1 tbsp sugar
4 ripe tomatoes, skinned, seeded and
    chopped, or 400g/14oz can tomatoes
juice of 1 lime
salt and ground black pepper
chopped fresh dill, to garnish

This light and refreshing lobster soup is ideal as an appetizer.
It is important to keep the shells as well as the flesh as they
impart additional flavour to the soup. Serve with crispbreads.

1 Remove the lobster meat from the shell (see page 20), reserving the shell. Set
the meat aside. Melt the butter in a pan, add the shallot, peppers, ginger and
garlic and cook for 5 minutes. Add the shell and cook gently for 10 minutes.

2 Add the brandy to the pan and set alight. Stir in the tomato purée. Add 1.25
litres/2¼ pints/5½ cups water, season lightly with salt and pepper, and bring
slowly to the boil. Lower the heat and simmer very gently for 40 minutes.

3 Strain the mixture into a clean pan. Add the vinegar, sugar, tomatoes and lime
juice to taste, and season necessary. Divide the lobster meat between four bowls.
Bring the soup to the boil then pour over the lobster. Serve garnished with
chopped dill.

Energy 275kcal/1155kJ; Protein 29.6g; Carbohydrate 14.1g, of which sugars 13.5g; Fat 7.8g, of which saturates 3.7g; Cholesterol
151mg; Calcium 99mg; Fibre 2.6g; Sodium 479mg.

CRAYFISH CHOWDER

SERVES 6

1kg/2¼lb live crayfish
75ml/5 tbsp vegetable oil
1 large tomato, diced
6 medium floury potatoes, peeled and
  cut into chunks
250g/9oz butternut squash, cut into
  cubes
250g/9oz/1½ cups shelled and skinned
  broad/fava beans
100g/3¾oz/½ cup long grain rice
2 corn cobs, cut into chunks
7.5ml/1½ tsp salt
6 eggs
350ml/12fl oz/1½ cups evaporated milk

COOK'S TIP

As crayfish eat anything on the ocean floor they must be purged before cooking. See page 23 for instructions.

Energy 466kcal/1956kJ; Protein 38.2g; Carbohydrate 41.5g, of which sugars 5.9g; Fat 17.1g, of which saturates 2.9g; Cholesterol 365mg; Calcium 119mg; Fibre 4.4g; Sodium 426mg.

This chunky soup recipe comes from Peru, and it is packed with vegetables – potatoes, butternut squash, broad beans and corn. Rice is added to thicken the soup and it's served topped with whole sweet crayfish and a poached egg. The crayfish will need to be purged 24 hours ahead of cooking.

1 Bring a large pan of water to the boil. Add the crayfish to the water and boil for 3–5 minutes until they change colour. Remove from the pan, reserving the stock, dry with kitchen paper and set aside.

2 Heat the oil in a large pan over high heat and add the tomato. Cook for 2 minutes, stirring, then add the stock.

3 Add the potato, butternut squash, beans, rice, corn and salt to the pan. Bring to the boil, then lower the heat and simmer for 15 minutes, until the potatoes are almost cooked.

4 Break the eggs into the hot soup, taking care that each one stays separate from the others. Simmer for 10–15 minutes, then remove from the heat. Stir in the milk and serve, distributing the crayfish evenly and adding a poached egg to each bowl.

CRAB AND CHILLI SOUP WITH FRESH CORIANDER RELISH

SERVES 4
45ml/3 tbsp olive oil
1 red onion, finely chopped
2 red chillies, seeded and chopped
1 garlic clove, finely chopped
450g/1lb cooked white crab meat
30ml/2 tbsp chopped fresh parsley
30ml/2 tbsp chopped fresh coriander/
   cilantro
juice of 2 lemons
1 lemon grass stalk
1 litre/1¾ pints/4 cups fish stock
15ml/1 tbsp Thai fish sauce (nam pla)
150g/5oz vermicelli or angel hair pasta,
   broken into 5–7.5cm/2–3in lengths
salt and ground black pepper

For the coriander relish
50g/2oz/1 cup fresh coriander/cilantro
   leaves
1 green chilli, seeded and chopped
15ml/1 tbsp sunflower oil
25ml/1½ tbsp lemon juice
2.5ml/½ tsp ground roasted cumin
   seeds

This Thai-inspired soup uses fresh white crab meat, lemon grass and Thai fish sauce, plus pasta to make it substantial enough to serve as a main course. It is accompanied by a hot coriander and green chilli relish.

1 Heat the oil in a pan and add the onion, chillies and garlic. Cook over a gentle heat for 10 minutes until the onion is soft. Transfer to a bowl and stir in the crab meat, parsley, coriander and lemon juice, then set aside.

2 Crush the lemon grass with a rolling pin. Pour the stock and fish sauce into a pan. Add the lemon grass and bring to the boil, then add the pasta. Simmer, uncovered, for 3–4 minutes or according to the packet instructions, until the pasta is just tender.

3 Meanwhile, make the coriander relish. Place the fresh coriander, chilli, oil, lemon juice and cumin in a food processor or blender and process to form a coarse paste. Season to taste.

4 Remove and discard the lemon grass. Stir the chilli and crab mixture into the soup and season. Bring to the boil, reduce the heat and simmer for 2 minutes. Ladle the soup into four warmed bowls and put a spoonful of the relish in each. Serve at once.

Energy 425kcal/1773kJ; Protein 26.7g; Carbohydrate 50.7g, of which sugars 1.4g; Fat 12.6g, of which saturates 1.6g; Cholesterol 81mg; Calcium 198mg; Fibre 1.1g; Sodium 767mg.

CRAB SOUP

SERVES 4–6
25g/1oz/2 tbsp unsalted butter
1 medium onion, finely chopped
1 celery stick, finely chopped
1 garlic clove, crushed
25ml/1½ tbsp plain/all purpose flour
225g/8oz cooked crab meat, half brown
  and half white
1.2 litres/2 pints/5 cups fish stock
150ml/¼ pint/⅔ cup double/heavy
  cream
30ml/2 tbsp dry sherry
salt and ground black pepper

Energy 209kcal/867kJ; Protein 7.8g; Carbohydrate 4.6g, of
which sugars 1.2g; Fat 17.3g, of which saturates 10.6g;
Cholesterol 70mg; Calcium 69mg; Fibre 0.3g; Sodium 241mg.

Although crab is available all the year round, it is at its best and is least expensive during the summer months – the perfect time to make this lovely, rich soup. It's made with brown and white crab meat, fish stock and sherry. Serve it with crusty white bread as a starter for a dinner party.

1 Melt the butter in a pan and add the onion, celery and garlic. Cook over a medium heat for about 5 minutes, stirring frequently, until the vegetables are soft but not browned.

2 Remove from the heat and quickly stir in the flour, then the brown crab meat. Gradually stir in the stock.

3 Bring the mixture just to the boil, then reduce the heat and simmer for about 30 minutes. Process or blend the soup and return it to the cleaned pan. Season to taste with salt and pepper.

4 Chop the white crab meat and stir it into the pan with the cream and sherry. Reheat the soup and serve immediately.

CHUNKY SEAFOOD CHUPE

SERVES 6

12 raw king prawns/jumbo shrimp,
   with shells
12 large live mussels
12 live clams
12 small scallops
12 small squid, cleaned
45ml/3 tbsp vegetable oil
1 medium red onion, finely chopped
2 large red/bell peppers, sliced
   lengthways
250g/9oz/1¼ cups long grain rice,
   washed and drained
250g/9oz/2 cups fresh or frozen peas
1 whole chilli
large bunch of coriander/cilantro,
   chopped
4 litres/7 pints/16 cups water
salt

Energy 329kcal/1374kJ; Protein 20.7g; Carbohydrate 43.8g, of
which sugars 5.3g; Fat 7.9g, of which saturates 1g; Cholesterol
135mg; Calcium 83mg; Fibre 3.5g; Sodium 193mg.

Chowders, known as chupes in South America, are an essential part of the cuisine in coastal regions as they use whatever fresh seafood is available such as prawns, mussels and clams.

1 Remove the heads of the king prawns and devein them by making a shallow cut down the back of each prawn. Using the tip of the knife, pull out and discard the dark intestinal tract. Scrub and rinse the mussels and clams well. Discard any mussel or clam shells that are open and do not close when sharply tapped. Clean the scallops by removing the elastic part around the shell and the brown part around the scallop. Slice the squid into rings.

2 Heat the oil in a large, deep pan and fry the onion for 10 minutes until it softens, add the red pepper, rice and peas and stir. Add the whole chilli.

3 Add 4 litres/7 pints/16 cups water to the pan and bring to the boil. Add the mussels to the pan together with the clams. Add the coriander. Season with salt, bring back to the boil and simmer for 10–12 minutes, until the rice has cooked. Discard any mussels or clams which have not fully opened.

4 Add the squid, scallops and prawns and fold into the rice. Simmer for another 3 minutes. Distribute evenly among the bowls to serve.

CORN AND CRAB SOUP

This dish is believed to have originated in Java, where at some time it was copied from the Chinese immigrants. It is now a well-loved soup throughout the Indonesian islands, eaten whenever fresh local crab are plentiful. It makes a delicious appetizer, or a light lunch with bread. A dash of vinegar adds piquancy to the richness of the egg and crab meat.

1 Combine the stock, creamed corn, salt and sesame oil in a large, heavy pan and bring the mixture to the boil.

2 Simmer for 5 minutes, then shred the crab meat and add to the pan. Gently cook for about 3 minutes.

3 Lightly beat the eggs and add to the barely simmering soup, stirring quickly to distribute the egg evenly and thicken the soup.

4 Adjust the seasoning and serve garnished with spring onions, with a dish of black vinegar on the side.

COOK'S TIPS
• Nothing quite matches the flavour of fresh crab meat, but Scandinavian canned crab or frozen crab are acceptable substitutes when fresh is not available.
• Black vinegar is made from fermented rice, millet, wheat, sorghum and barley. If you are unable to find it, use a dash of balsamic vinegar instead.

SERVES 4
750ml/1¼ pints/3 cups seafood stock
450g/1lb can creamed corn
5ml/1 tsp salt
15ml/1 tbsp sesame oil
250g/9oz cooked white crab meat
2 eggs
2 spring onions/scallions,
   trimmed and sliced, to garnish
black vinegar, to serve

Energy 279kcal/1173kJ; Protein 18.6g; Carbohydrate 29.9g, of which sugars 10.8g; Fat 10.3g, of which saturates 1.9g; Cholesterol 140mg; Calcium 19mg; Fibre 1.6g; Sodium 1093mg.

CRAB AND ASPARAGUS SOUP WITH NUOC CHAM

This fragrant soup recipe has been adapted from the classic French asparagus velouté to produce a meatier version that has more texture. Brown, white or a mixture of both types of crab meat can be used.

SERVES 4
15ml/1 tbsp vegetable oil
2 shallots, finely chopped
2 garlic cloves, finely chopped
15ml/1 tbsp rice flour or cornflour/
  cornstarch
450g/1lb asparagus, trimmed
225g/8oz cooked crab meat
salt and ground black pepper
basil and coriander/cilantro leaves, to
  garnish
Vietnamese dipping sauce (nuoc cham),
  to serve

For the stock
1 meaty chicken carcass
25g/1oz dried shrimps, soaked in water
  for 30 minutes, rinsed and drained
2 onions, peeled and quartered
2 garlic cloves, crushed
15ml/1 tbsp nuoc cham
6 black peppercorns
sea salt

1 To make the stock, put the chicken carcass into a deep pan. Add all the other stock ingredients, except the salt, and pour in 2 litres/3½ pints/8 cups water. Bring to the boil, boil for a few minutes, skim off any foam, reduce the heat then simmer, covered, for 1½–2 hours. Remove the lid and simmer for a further 30 minutes to reduce the stock. Skim off any fat, season with salt, strain and measure out 1.5 litres/2½ pints/6¼ cups.

2 Heat the oil in a wok. Stir in the shallots and garlic, until they begin to colour. Remove from the heat, stir in the flour, and then the stock. Return to the heat and bring to the boil, stirring constantly, until smooth.

3 Steam the asparagus until just tender. Add the crab meat and asparagus to the soup, reduce the heat and simmer for 15–20 minutes. Season, then serve, garnished with basil and coriander, and a splash of nuoc cham.

Energy 142kcal/590kJ; Protein 17.1g; Carbohydrate 6.9g, of which sugars 3g; Fat 5.1g, of which saturates 0.6g; Cholesterol 72mg; Calcium 177mg; Fibre 2.1g; Sodium 584mg.

CAPPUCCINO OF LOBSTER, PUY LENTILS AND TARRAGON

This is a sophisticated lobster soup, which any guest would find hugely impressive as an appetizer. Adding the ice cold butter a little at a time is what gives the soup its light frothy texture.

SERVES 6

450g/1lb cooked lobster meat, cut into small pieces
150g/5oz/⅔ cup Puy lentils
1 carrot, halved
1 celery stick, halved
1 small onion, halved
1 garlic clove
1 bay leaf
large bunch of tarragon, tied firmly
1 litre/1¾ pints/4 cups lobster or fish stock
120ml/4fl oz/½ cup double/heavy cream
25g/1oz/2 tbsp unsalted butter, finely diced and chilled until ice cold
salt and ground black pepper
fresh tarragon sprigs and lobster claws (if available), to garnish

COOK'S TIP
Plan to serve this soup immediately, otherwise the froth will disappear.

1 Put the cooked lobster and the lentils in a pan and cover with cold water. Add the vegetables, garlic and herbs. Bring to the boil and simmer for 20 minutes. Drain the lentils and discard the vegetables and herbs. Purée the lentils in a food processor or blender until smooth. Set aside.

2 Pour the lobster or fish stock into a large clean pan and bring to the boil. Lightly stir in the lentil purée and cream, but do not mix too much at this point otherwise you will not be able to create the cappuccino effect. The mixture should still be quite watery. Season well.

3 Using either a hand-held blender or electric beater, whisk up the soup mixture, adding the butter one piece at a time, until it is very frothy. Divide the lobster meat among the bowls and carefully pour in the soup. Garnish with sprigs of tarragon and lobster claws (if available) and serve at once.

Energy 241kcal/1005kJ; Protein 13g; Carbohydrate 14g, of which sugars 2g; Fat 15g, of which saturates 9g; Cholesterol 66mg; Calcium 51mg; Fibre 0g; Sodium 325mg.

BLUE CRAB SOUP

This Korean recipe is usually made with blue crabs, but if these are not available any type will do. This is a flavoursome, healthy one-pot meal, almost a casserole, packed full of flavours and textures. Traditional ingredients such as Korean chilli powder and chrysanthemum leaves are available from specialist oriental shops.

SERVES 4

2 live blue crabs, about 150g/5oz each
7.5ml/1½ tsp sesame oil
15ml/1 tbsp Korean chilli powder
2 garlic cloves, crushed
300g/11oz Chinese white radish, peeled and diced
300g/11oz courgette/zucchini, thinly sliced
50g/2oz green chilli, seeded and sliced
20g/¾oz red chilli, seeded and sliced
5ml/1 tsp light soy sauce
5ml/1 tsp dark soy sauce
5ml/1 tsp salt
5ml/1 tsp sugar
275g/10oz leeks, roughly sliced
50g/2oz chrysanthemum leaves
50g/2oz watercress
15ml/1 tbsp doenjang soya bean paste
15ml/1 tbsp sake

1 Put the crabs in iced water for at least 20 minutes to stun them. Despatch the crabs following the instructions on page 22. Remove their top shells and small legs (set these aside). Remove the entrails, gills and mouth parts. Slit the crabs down the middle, using a heavy knife and a meat mallet.

2 Place the shells and legs in a large pan. Pour in 1.5 litres/2½ pints/6¼ cups water and bring to the boil. Reduce the heat and simmer for 1 hour, removing any scum, if necessary. Strain the stock, discarding the shells and legs.

3 Heat a large pan over a low heat and add 50ml/2fl oz/½ cup of the crab stock. Stir in the sesame oil, half the chilli powder and the garlic. Bring to the boil, then reduce the heat and simmer the mixture briefly. Add the rest of the stock and mix it with the chilli-flavoured stock. Add the radish. Bring back to the boil, then reduce the heat and simmer for 10 minutes.

4 Add the crab halves, courgette and green and red chillies, and boil for a further 10 minutes, until the crab turns bright orange. Add the remaining chilli powder, the soy sauces, salt and sugar and bring the soup back to the boil.

5 Add the leeks, chrysanthemum leaves, watercress, doenjang soya bean paste and sake. Remove the pan from the heat and cover it, then leave to stand for 2 minutes before serving.

Energy 168kcal/700kJ; Protein 20.5g; Carbohydrate 7g, of which sugars 6.3g; Fat 6.4g, of which saturates 0.9g; Cholesterol 63mg; Calcium 57mg; Fibre 3.4g; Sodium 1055mg.

APPETIZERS

It might be a hard act to follow, but a lobster or
crab makes a fabulous start to any meal. Prawns
are also a very popular ingredient for an appetizer
and in this chapter you will find a very tempting
selection of first course dishes.

POTTED LOBSTER

This dish dates back to before refrigeration, when encasing fish or meat in butter meant it would keep – and travel – for up to a month. This elegant version of potted shrimps works perfectly with lobster and makes a great appetizer.

SERVES 4
225g/8oz cooked lobster tails
225g/8oz/1 cup unsalted butter
pinch of ground mace
2.5ml/½ tsp cayenne pepper
dill sprigs, to garnish
lemon wedges and thin slices of brown
  bread, to serve
salt

Energy 461kcal/1901kJ; Protein 10.3g; Carbohydrate 0.4g, of which sugars 0.4g; Fat 46.6g, of which saturates 29.4g; Cholesterol 230mg; Calcium 55mg; Fibre 0g; Sodium 448mg.

1 Chop half of the lobster tails finely, and the other half roughly. Melt half the butter slowly, carefully skimming off any foam that rises to the surface with a metal spoon.

2 Stir all the chopped lobster, the mace, cayenne and salt, to taste, into the pan and heat gently without boiling. Pour the lobster and butter mixture into four individual pots or ramekins and leave to cool.

3 Heat the remaining butter in a clean small pan, then carefully spoon the clear butter over the lobster, leaving behind the sediment.

4 Leave until the butter is almost set, then place a dill sprig in the centre of each pot. Leave to set completely, then cover and chill. Transfer the pots to room temperature for 30 minutes before serving. Then serve with lemon wedges for squeezing over and thin slices of brown bread.

LOBSTER CAKES WITH TARTARE SAUCE

These light patties are a modern version of American Maryland crab cakes.
Ready-cooked lobster meat is combined with sherry, fresh herbs and mayo.
A chunky home-made tartare sauce is the ideal accompaniment.

SERVES 4
675g/1½lb cooked lobster meat
1 egg, beaten
30ml/2 tbsp mayonnaise
15ml/1 tbsp Worcestershire sauce
15ml/1 tbsp sherry
30ml/2 tbsp finely chopped parsley
15ml/1 tbsp finely chopped chives
45ml/3 tbsp olive oil
salt and ground black pepper

For the tartare sauce
1 egg yolk
15ml/1 tbsp white wine vinegar
30ml/2 tbsp Dijon mustard
250ml/8fl oz/1 cup vegetable oil
30ml/2 tbsp lemon juice
20g/¾oz/¼ cup finely chopped spring
   onions/scallions
30ml/2 tbsp chopped drained capers
few chopped gherkins/sour dill pickles
60ml/4 tbsp finely chopped parsley

1 Place the lobster meat in a food processor and pulse gradually until you have a rough mixture; don't over-blend, you need to retain some texture.

2 In a bowl, combine the beaten egg with the mayonnaise, Worcestershire sauce, sherry and herbs. Season with salt and pepper. Gently fold in the lobster.

3 Divide the mixture into eight equal portions and gently form each one into an oval cake. Place on a baking sheet between layers of baking parchment and chill for 1 hour.

4 Make the sauce. In a bowl, beat the egg yolk. Add the vinegar and mustard and season with salt and pepper, and whisk for 10 seconds. Gradually whisk in the oil in a slow, steady stream. Add the lemon juice, spring onions, capers, gherkins and parsley to the sauce and mix well. Check the seasoning. Cover and chill for 30 minutes.

5 Preheat the grill or broiler to high. Brush the lobster cakes with the olive oil. Place on an oiled baking sheet, in one layer. Grill the cakes 15cm/6in from the heat until golden brown, about 5 minutes on each side. Serve the lobster cakes hot with the tartare sauce.

Energy 710kcal/2934kJ; Protein 33.8g; Carbohydrate 1.9g, of which sugars 1.7g; Fat 62.6g, of which saturates 8.1g; Cholesterol 225mg; Calcium 234mg; Fibre 0.2g; Sodium 1249mg.

DUBLIN LAWYER

SERVES 2
800g/1¾lb cooked lobster in its shell
175g/6oz/¾ cup unsalted butter
75ml/2½fl oz/⅓ cup Irish whiskey
150ml/¼ pint/⅔ cup
  double/heavy cream
sea salt and ground black pepper

This classic Irish dish of lobster with whiskey and cream was traditionally made with raw lobster, but this version uses a ready-cooked one. The origins of the name are uncertain, but it is generally thought to refer to the fact that lawyers are more likely than most to be able to afford this luxurious dish.

1 Remove all the meat from the cooked lobster, following the instructions on page 20, and retain both half tail sections for serving. Cut all the meat into bite-sized pieces. Place the half shell sections in a very low oven to keep warm.

2 Melt the butter in a pan over a low heat. Add the lobster pieces and turn in the butter to warm through.

3 Warm the whiskey in a separate pan and pour it over the lobster. Carefully set it alight. When the flames have died down add the cream and heat gently without allowing the sauce to boil, then season to taste. Turn the hot mixture into the warm shells and serve immediately.

Energy 1273Kcal/5259kJ; Protein 37.8g; Carbohydrate 1.8g, of which sugars 1.8g; Fat 114.9g, of which saturates 71.1g; Cholesterol 469mg; Calcium 152mg; Fibre 0g; Sodium 108g.

CREAMY CRAB BAKE

SERVES 4
butter, for greasing
225g/8oz cooked white crab meat
juice of ½ lemon
15ml/1 tbsp chopped fresh herbs, such
   as parsley, chives or fennel
20ml/4 tsp gin
60ml/4 tbsp grated hard cheese, such
   as Parmesan
ground black pepper

For the béchamel sauce
1 small onion
3 cloves
300ml/½ pint/1¼ cups milk
½ bay leaf
25g/1oz/2 tbsp unsalted butter
25g/1oz/¼ cup plain/all-purpose flour
5ml/1 tsp smooth Dijon mustard
5ml/1 tsp wholegrain Dijon mustard

Energy 224Kcal/936kJ; Protein 17.4g; Carbohydrate 9.6g, of
which sugars 4.5g; Fat 11.9g, of which saturates 7.4g;
Cholesterol 73mg; Calcium 282mg; Fibre 0.4g; Sodium 489mg.

A simple combination of white crab meat, lemon juice and
fresh herbs is topped with béchamel sauce and grated cheese
and baked until golden. A slug of gin gives extra zing.

1 First make an infusion for the béchamel sauce: stud the onion with the cloves,
and then put it into a small pan with the milk and bay leaf. Bring slowly to the
boil, then allow to infuse or steep for 15 minutes, and strain.

2 Preheat the oven to 180°C/350°F/Gas 4 and butter four gratin dishes. Toss the
crab meat in the lemon juice. Divide it among the dishes and add a pinch of
herbs to each. Sprinkle each dish with 5ml/1 tsp gin, and a little pepper.

3 Melt the butter for the sauce in a pan, stir in the flour and cook over
a low heat for 1–2 minutes. Gradually add the infused milk, stirring constantly
to make a smooth sauce. Simmer over a low heat for 1–2 minutes.

4 Blend the béchamel sauce with the two mustards and use to cover the crab.
Sprinkle the cheese on top, and bake for 20–25 minutes, until hot and bubbling.

COOK'S TIP
The recipe can also be divided between two larger dishes to serve two as a main
course with a large green salad and crusty bread.

LOBSTER AND FILO TART

Tarts are a very popular appetizer, and a moreish lobster filling encased in a light and airy filo pastry is certain to start off any meal well. Make the tart in advance and heat gently for 10 minutes before serving, if you wish.

SERVES 4–6

2 eggs, beaten

150ml/¼ pint/⅔ cup milk

200g/7oz cooked lobster meat, chopped into small pieces

200g/7oz cooked prawns, peeled and deveined

225g/8oz/1 cup curd cheese

115g/4oz/2 cups mushrooms, chopped

10 filo pastry sheets

50g/2oz/¼ cup unsalted butter, melted

salt and ground black pepper

50g/2oz/⅔ cup Parmesan cheese shavings, to garnish

1 Preheat the oven to 190°C/375°F/Gas 5. Grease a deep 18cm/7in flan tin. Mix together the eggs, milk, lobster meat, prawns, curd cheese and mushrooms in a bowl. Season to taste with salt and pepper.

2 Line the flan tin with filo pastry, placing the sheets at alternate angles and brushing each one with a little of the melted butter. Leave the excess pastry hanging over the sides of the tin.

3 Spoon the filling into the filo-lined tin. Fold the excess pastry over, crumpling it slightly to make a decorative edge. Brush with melted butter. Bake the tart for 35–40 minutes. Scatter the Parmesan cheese over. Cut into wedges to serve.

COOK'S TIP
Work quickly with filo pastry as it soon becomes dry and brittle. Cover any filo not actually being used with a damp, clean dish towel.

Energy 644kcal/2685kJ; Protein 28.1g; Carbohydrate 46.3g, of which sugars 3.3g; Fat 39.8g, of which saturates 23g; Cholesterol 278mg; Calcium 288mg; Fibre 2.4g; Sodium 609mg.

HOT AND SPICY CRAB CLAWS

SERVES 4
50g/2oz/½ cup rice flour
15ml/1 tbsp cornflour/cornstarch
2.5ml/½ tsp sugar
1 egg
1 lemon grass stalk, root trimmed
2 garlic cloves, finely chopped
15ml/1 tbsp chopped fresh
   coriander/cilantro
1–2 fresh red chillies, seeded and finely
   chopped
5ml/1 tsp Thai fish sauce (nam pla)
vegetable oil, for frying
12 half-shelled cooked crab claws
ground black pepper

For the chilli vinegar dip
45ml/3 tbsp sugar
120ml/4fl oz/½ cup red wine vinegar
15ml/1 tbsp Thai fish sauce (nam pla)
2–4 fresh red chillies, seeded
   and chopped

Crab claws are readily available in the freezer cabinet in many Asian stores and supermarkets. Thaw out thoroughly and dry on kitchen paper before dipping in the batter.

1 Make the chilli dip. Mix the sugar and 120ml/4fl oz/½ cup water in a pan, stirring until the sugar has dissolved, then bring to the boil. Lower the heat and simmer for 5–7 minutes. Stir in the rest of the ingredients and set aside.

2 Combine the rice flour, cornflour and sugar in a bowl. Beat the egg with 60ml/4 tbsp cold water, then add the egg and water mixture into the flour mixture and beat well until it forms a light batter.

3 Cut off the lower 5cm/2in of the lemon grass stalk and chop it finely. Add the lemon grass to the batter, with the garlic, coriander, red chillies, fish sauce and pepper to taste.

4 Heat the oil in a wok or deep-fryer. Pat the crab claws dry and dip into the batter. Drop the battered claws into the hot oil, a few at a time. Fry until golden brown. Using a slotted spoon, lift the claws out, drain on kitchen paper and keep hot. Pour the dip into a serving bowl and serve with the hot crab claws.

Energy 224kcal/933kJ; Protein 10.1g; Carbohydrate 16.9g, of which sugars 0g; Fat 12.9g, of which saturates 1.7g; Cholesterol 78mg; Calcium 62mg; Fibre 0.3g; Sodium 256mg.

DRUNKEN PRAWNS

SERVES 6

60ml/4 tbsp extra virgin olive oil
3 garlic cloves, finely chopped
½ onion, finely chopped
1 green/bell pepper, cut into cubes
30ml/2 tbsp chopped basil, plus some
    extra basil leaves to serve
30ml/2 tbsp chopped fresh parsley
1kg/2¼lb raw king prawns/jumbo
    shrimp, with shells
120ml/4fl oz/ ½ cup Cognac
120ml/4fl oz/ ½ cup cold water

In this traditional recipe from southern Italy, plump and juicy shell-on prawns are cooked with garlic, onion, basil, parsley and green pepper. The 'drunken' part of the recipe comes from a generous measure of brandy, which adds a wonderful flavour and aroma to the finished dish. Serve with plenty of rustic bread to mop up the tasty sauce.

1 Heat the olive oil in a large pan, add the garlic, onion and green pepper, and fry over a medium heat, stirring frequently, until the pepper has softened. Add the basil and parsley to the pan and stir through.

2 Add the prawns to the pan and turn gently to coat them with the oil. Continue to cook until they have started to turn pink.

Energy 192kcal/798kJ; Protein 15g; Carbohydrate 2.9g, of which sugars 2.5g; Fat 8.7g, of which saturates 1.4g; Cholesterol 52mg; Calcium 113mg; Fibre 1g; Sodium 1021mg.

3 Add the Cognac and 120ml/4fl oz/½ cup water to the pan. Simmer for 5 minutes, then serve, sprinkled with a few extra basil leaves.

One of the best ways to enjoy these big beautiful prawns is to coat them in a simple batter and deep-fry until crisp. Cut the tails into fantails, if you wish, for an extra presentational flourish. You will find the instructions for this on page 24.

KING PRAWNS IN CRISPY BATTER

SERVES 4
120ml/4fl oz/½ cup water
1 egg
115g/4oz/1 cup plain/all-purpose flour
5ml/1 tsp cayenne pepper
12 raw king prawns/jumbo shrimp, with shells
vegetable oil, for deep frying
sea salt
flat leaf parsley, to garnish and lemon wedges, to serve (optional)

1 In a large bowl, whisk together 120ml/4fl oz/½ cup water and the egg. Whisk in the flour and cayenne pepper until smooth.

2 Peel the prawns, leaving just the tails intact. Make a shallow cut down the back of each prawn. Using the tip of the knife, pull out and discard the dark intestinal tract.

3 Heat the oil in a large pan or deep-fat fryer, until a cube of bread dropped into the oil browns in 1 minute.

4 Holding the prawns by their tails, dip them into the batter, one at a time, shaking off any excess. Carefully drop each prawn into the oil and fry for 2–3 minutes until crisp and golden. Drain on kitchen paper then place into bowls and sprinkle over with sea salt. Garnish with parsley and serve with lemon wedges, if you like.

VARIATION
If you have any batter left over, use it to coat thin strips of vegetables such as sweet potato, beetroot/beet, carrot or pepper.

Energy 253kcal/1061kJ; Protein 13.1g; Carbohydrate 22.4g, of which sugars 0.4g; Fat 13.1g, of which saturates 1.8g; Cholesterol 145mg; Calcium 87mg; Fibre 0.9g; Sodium 113mg.

KING PRAWNS AND BEEF ORIENTAL SALAD

In this sophisticated appetizer, succulent steamed prawns are mixed with shredded beef and crunchy bamboo shoots, then coated with a rich dressing of pine nuts. It can be prepared, cooked and chilled up to 24 hours in advance and arranged on platters just before serving.

SERVES 2

6 raw king prawns/jumbo shrimp, with shells
20g/¾oz fresh root ginger, peeled and sliced
15ml/1 tbsp mirin or rice wine
½ cucumber
75g/3oz bamboo shoots, sliced
90g/3½oz beef flank, cooked
15ml/1 tbsp vegetable oil
salt

For the dressing
60ml/4 tbsp pine nuts
10ml/2 tsp sesame oil
ground black pepper

1 Prepare a steamer over a pan of boiling water, with a bowl in place under the steamer to catch any liquid. Place the prawns in the steamer with the ginger, and pour over the mirin or rice wine. Steam for 8 minutes.

2 Seed the cucumber and slice it lengthways into thin strips. Sprinkle with salt, and then leave to stand for 5 minutes. Squeeze the cucumber gently to remove any liquid.

3 Remove the prawns from the steamer, discarding the ginger. Remove the bowl of liquid from beneath the steamer and set it aside.

4 Blanch the bamboo shoots in boiling water for 30 seconds. Remove, slice and sprinkle with salt. Add the beef to the boiling water and cook until tender. Drain and leave to cool.

5 Make a shallow cut down the back of each prawn. Using the tip of the knife, pull out and discard the dark intestinal tract. Rinse the prawns thoroughly. Slice them into 2cm/½in pieces. Transfer to the refrigerator.

6 Slice the beef thinly, cut into bitesize pieces and chill in the refrigerator. Coat a frying pan or wok with the vegetable oil and quickly stir-fry the cucumber and bamboo shoots, then chill them.

7 To make the dressing, roughly grind the pine nuts in a mortar and pestle and then transfer to a bowl. Add 45ml/3 tbsp of the prawn liquid from the bowl and add the sesame oil with a pinch of salt and pepper. Mix well.

8 Arrange all the chilled ingredients on a platter and pour over the dressing before serving.

Energy 416kcal/1724kJ; Protein 24.7g; Carbohydrate 3.5g, of which sugars 2.7g; Fat 33.8g, of which saturates 4.3g; Cholesterol 124mg; Calcium 62mg; Fibre 1.5g; Sodium 619mg.

SALADS, BURGERS AND BITES

Lobster and crab don't have to be served as part of a
sumptuous dinner party, they can also make great
snacks and light meals. In coastal areas where
shellfish are plentiful crab sandwiches or a turf and
surf burger are everyday fare.

WARM BABY NEW POTATO AND LOBSTER SALAD

This flavour-packed main course salad is perfect for an easy summer lunch or supper, and can also be made in advance: simply assemble, refrigerate and then dress at the last minute. Serve with a well-chilled dry white wine.

SERVES 4

750g/1lb 10oz baby new potatoes
125g/4¼oz fine green beans, trimmed
2 lemon slices
bunch of flat leaf parsley
4 raw lobster tails, shell on
100g/3¾oz wild rocket/arugula
12 sun-dried tomatoes in oil, drained
    and roughly chopped
bunch of fresh basil, leaves only
salt and ground black pepper

For the dressing

75ml/5 tbsp extra virgin olive oil
15ml/1 tbsp oil from a jar of sun-dried
    tomatoes
60ml/4 tbsp white balsamic vinegar
15ml/1 tbsp clear honey
15ml/1 tbsp wholegrain mustard

1 Place the potatoes in a medium pan of salted water over a high heat. Bring to the boil and cook for 10 minutes. Add the beans and boil for a further 5 minutes or until the potatoes are cooked and the beans are just tender. Drain and cover with the lid to keep hot.

2 Meanwhile, pour 2.5cm/1in water into another medium pan and add the lemon slices and parsley. Bring the water to the boil and then add the lobster tails, shell side down. Reduce the heat, cover and simmer gently for 8–10 minutes or until the flesh is firm and opaque. The lobster shells will turn a dark red colour.

3 Using a slotted spoon, remove the lobster tails from the pan and reserve the cooking stock. Place the tails shell side down on a plate and, using sharp kitchen scissors or poultry shears, cut through the underside of the body and gently pull the shell away.

4 Using a sharp knife remove the dark black thread that runs along the length of the tail. Chop the lobster meat into bite-sized pieces.

5 To make the dressing, whisk the oils, vinegar, honey and mustard in a small bowl, season and stir well.

6 Transfer the potatoes and beans to a serving bowl, add the rocket, tomatoes and basil and plenty of ground black pepper. Pour the dressing over and toss to coat. Place the lobster meat on top of the salad and serve.

COOK'S TIP
Strain the reserved stock and allow it to cool to room temperature, then chill in the refrigerator for up to 2 days or freeze for up to 1 month.

Energy 532kcal/2216kJ; Protein 16.1g; Carbohydrate 36.5g, of which sugars 7.6g; Fat 36.8g, of which saturates 5.2g; Cholesterol 112mg; Calcium 126mg; Fibre 5g; Sodium 566mg.

HOT LOBSTER BRIOCHE ROLLS

SERVES 4
2 lemon slices, plus juice of ½ lemon
2 sprigs of flat leaf parsley, plus
   30ml/2 tbsp chopped flat leaf parsley
4 raw lobster tails, shell on
40g/1½oz butter
2 garlic cloves, finely chopped
4 brioche rolls
1 little gem/Bibb lettuce, roughly
   chopped
ground black pepper

These are no ordinary rolls. Lightly steamed lobster is mixed with hot lemon, garlic and parsley butter and divided between soft brioche rolls. Add plenty of black pepper and some crispy lettuce and that's all there is to it. For an upmarket treat this New England classic can't be beaten.

1 Pour 2.5cm/1in water into a medium pan and add the lemon slices and parsley sprigs. Bring the water to the boil and then add the lobster tails, shell side down. Reduce the heat, cover and simmer gently for 8–10 minutes or until the flesh is firm and opaque. The lobster shells will turn a dark red colour.

2 Meanwhile, melt the butter in a small pan over a low heat and add the garlic. Cook gently for 5 minutes. Stir in the chopped parsley and lemon juice and season well with freshly ground black pepper. Keep warm over a very low heat.

3 Using a slotted spoon, remove the tails from the pan and reserve the cooking stock to use for another recipe. Place the tails shell side down on a plate and, using sharp kitchen scissors or poultry shears, cut through the underside of the body and gently pull the shell away. Using a sharp knife remove the dark black thread that runs along the length of the tail.

4 Roughly chop the lobster meat and add to the butter mixture. Stir to combine.

5 Split and lightly toast the cut side of the rolls. Divide the lettuce between the rolls and add one-quarter of the lobster mixture to each one. Grind on some black pepper, add the tops of the buns, and serve immediately.

Energy 240kcal/1006kJ; Protein 14.6g; Carbohydrate 23.7g, of which sugars 1.6g; Fat 10.3g, of which saturates 5.6g; Cholesterol 71mg; Calcium 130mg; Fibre 1.9g; Sodium 454mg.

CITRUS LOBSTER WRAPS

Buying meaty lobster tails rather than a whole lobster makes cooking and preparation much easier. Here they are steamed with lime and coriander then combined with avocado, creamy Greek yogurt and red pepper to make a great filling for wraps. This filling is equally good served on crackers as canapés or to top baked potatoes.

SERVES 4

2 lime slices plus the juice of 1 lime

3 sprigs of fresh coriander/cilantro, plus 60ml/4 tbsp roughly chopped fresh coriander/cilantro

4 raw lobster tails, shell on

2 ripe avocados, roughly chopped

100ml/3½fl oz/scant ½ cup Greek/strained plain yogurt

1 red/bell pepper, deseeded and very finely chopped

4 wraps

salt and ground black pepper

1 Pour 2.5cm/1in water into a medium pan and add the lime slices and coriander sprigs. Bring the water to the boil and then add the lobster tails, shell side down. Reduce the heat, cover and simmer gently for 8–10 minutes or until the flesh is firm and opaque. The lobster shells will turn a dark red colour.

2 Meanwhile, place the avocados in a medium bowl and mash using a fork – the mixture needs to be spreadable, but retain a little texture. Stir in the yogurt, lime juice, coriander and red pepper and season to taste with salt and black pepper. Cover and set aside.

3 Using a slotted spoon, remove the tails from the pan and reserve the cooking stock to use for another recipe. Place the tails shell side down on a plate and, using sharp kitchen scissors or poultry shears, cut through the underside of the body and gently pull the shell away. Using a sharp knife remove the dark black thread that runs along the length of the tail. Roughly chop the lobster meat.

4 Spread one-quarter of the avocado mixture across the centre of each wrap and top with one-quarter of the lobster. Roll the wraps up, cut in half and serve straight away.

Energy 329kcal/1380kJ; Protein 17.2g; Carbohydrate 35.5g, of which sugars 5.3g; Fat 14.1g, of which saturates 4g; Cholesterol 54mg; Calcium 176mg; Fibre 6.6g; Sodium 323mg.

SURF AND TURF BURGERS

A twist on the classic seafood and meat combination – these burgers are topped with easy-to-cook lobster tails in a chive and lemon mayo. Try them for a weekend family lunch served with skin-on potato wedges.

SERVES 4

For the burgers
450g/1lb minced/ground beef
100g/3¾oz/2 cups fresh white
  breadcrumbs
2 garlic cloves, very finely chopped
1 small red onion, very finely chopped
1 egg
5ml/1 tsp Worcestershire sauce
5ml/1 tsp Dijon mustard
30ml/2 tbsp olive oil
salt and ground black pepper

For the lobster
1 lemon slice
bunch of fresh chives
2 raw lobster tails, shell on
45ml/3 tbsp mayonnaise
10ml/2 tsp lemon juice

To serve
4 brioche or burger buns
30ml/2 tbsp mayonnaise
1 beefsteak tomato, sliced into 4
4 romaine lettuce leaves, roughly torn

COOK'S TIP
The reserved lobster stock can be used
in a variety of recipes. Strain, and
allow it to cool to room temperature,
then chill in the refrigerator for up to
2 days or freeze for up to 1 month.

1 To make the burgers, place all the ingredients, except the oil, in a large mixing bowl. Season and stir well to thoroughly combine. Divide into 4 equal portions and with damp hands shape into burgers. Place on a baking tray and chill in the refrigerator for 1 hour.

2 Pour 2.5cm/1in water into a medium pan and add the lemon slice and three-quarters of the chives. Bring the water to the boil and then add the lobster tails, shell side down. Reduce the heat, cover and simmer gently for 8–10 minutes or until the flesh is firm and opaque. The lobster shells will turn a dark red colour.

3 Meanwhile, chop the remaining chives and mix with the mayonnaise, lemon juice and plenty of freshly ground black pepper.

4 Using a slotted spoon, remove the tails from the pan and reserve the cooking stock. Place the tails shell side down on a plate and, using sharp kitchen scissors or poultry shears, cut through the underside of the body and gently pull the shell away. Using a sharp knife remove the dark black thread that runs along the length of the tail.

5 Roughly chop the lobster meat and add to the chive and lemon mayonnaise. Stir well to combine, cover and set aside.

6 Heat the oil in large non-stick frying pan over a medium-high heat and cook the burgers for 4–5 minutes on each side.

7 Split and lightly toast the cut side of the buns. Spread the bottom half of each bun with some mayonnaise and add a tomato slice and some lettuce. Place the cooked burgers on top and spoon one-quarter of the lobster mixture over each burger. Top with the bun halves and serve immediately.

Energy 693kcal/2892kJ; Protein 36.6g; Carbohydrate 40.8g, of which sugars 4.6g; Fat 43.8g, of which saturates 12g; Cholesterol 176mg; Calcium 182mg; Fibre 3.7g; Sodium 709mg.

CRAB, HORSERADISH AND BEETROOT SALAD

In this beautifully flavoured salad the piquant combination of grated vegetables and horseradish complement the sweet, fresh crab meat perfectly.

SERVES 4

200g/7oz raw beetroot/beets, grated
300g/11oz mooli/daikon, grated
115g/4oz carrots, grated
30ml/2 tbsp sour cream
15ml/1 tbsp creamed horseradish
30ml/2 tbsp mayonnaise
45ml/3 tbsp finely chopped fresh dill
115g/4oz cooked white crab meat
grated rind and juice of 1 lemon
115g/4oz small beetroot/beet leaves, or
   rocket/arugula
salt and ground black pepper

1 Wrap the grated beetroot in a piece of muslin or cheesecloth and squeeze out as much liquid as possible. Put the beetroot into a large bowl and add the grated mooli and carrots.

2 Add the soured cream, creamed horseradish and mayonnaise, then mix well. Sprinkle with the dill and gently stir into the salad. Season to taste and chill until ready to serve.

3 Put the crab meat into a bowl and add the lemon rind and juice. Mix and season. When ready to serve, put a 12cm/4½in metal ring in the middle of a plate, then put a small handful of beetroot leaves or rocket into the ring.

4 Spoon in the mooli, horseradish and beetroot salad, gently pressing down, then remove the ring. Repeat for the remaining plates. Scoop a generous spoonful of the crab meat on to the top of the salads and serve immediately.

Energy 154kcal/640kJ; Protein 8.4g; Carbohydrate 9.1g, of which sugars 8.4g; Fat 9.6g, of which saturates 2.2g; Cholesterol 31mg; Calcium 90mg; Fibre 3g; Sodium 281mg.

DRESSED CRAB
WITH ASPARAGUS

This is a classic way to serve crab, and one of the best ways to make the most of it when it is fresh from the sea. Dressed crabs have been freshly cooked by the fishmonger and the crab meat placed back inside the shell.

1 Wash the asparagus and trim off the bases. Boil in a pan of water for about 7 minutes, until you can spear a stem with the blade of a knife and the blade slips out easily. Plunge the spears into iced water to stop them from cooking any further. Drain them when cold, and pat dry with kitchen paper.

2 Scoop out the white crab meat from the shells and claws and place it in a bowl. If you can't find fresh crabs, you can use the same amount of canned or frozen white crab meat (about 800g/1¾lb). Ensure the meat is completely defrosted and place on to kitchen paper to dry.

SERVES 4
24 asparagus spears
4 dressed crabs
30ml/2 tbsp mayonnaise
15ml/1 tbsp chopped fresh parsley
Tabasco sauce and toast, to serve

3 Add the mayonnaise and chopped fresh parsley to the bowl and combine with the crab meat. Place the mixture into the crab shells and add a few asparagus spears per serving. Serve with a few drops of Tabasco sauce and warm slices of crisp toast.

Per portion Energy 207kcal/859kJ; Protein 19.5g; Carbohydrate 3g, of which sugars 2.8g; Fat 13g, of which saturates 1.9g; Cholesterol 72mg; Calcium 157mg; Fibre 2.6g; Sodium 540mg.

CRAB MEAT SALAD WITH GARLIC DRESSING

SERVES 2–3

45ml/3 tbsp sugar
30ml/2 tbsp cider vinegar
30ml/2 tbsp pineapple juice
5ml/1 tsp grated fresh root ginger
1 Asian pear, cored and finely sliced
1 cucumber, peeled, seeded and finely
  sliced
10ml/2 tsp cornflour/cornstarch
150g/5oz cooked white and brown crab
  meat
20g/¾oz cress, to garnish

For the dressing
30ml/2 tbsp Dijon mustard
30ml/2 tbsp white wine vinegar
2 garlic cloves, crushed
15ml/1 tbsp pineapple juice
5ml/1 tsp dark soy sauce
5ml/1 tsp salt
30ml/2 tbsp sugar

The combination of finely sliced Asian pear and cucumber makes a light, refreshing contrast to the sweetness of the steamed crab in this salad. A simple dressing with garlic, pineapple juice and soy sauce complements the flavours and a sprinkling of cress adds a subtle peppery finish.

1 Combine the sugar, cider vinegar, pineapple juice and ginger in a bowl. Add 1.5 litres/2½ pints/6¼ cups chilled water and stir gently until the sugar has dissolved. Add the Asian pear and cucumber and leave for 10 minutes, then drain and set aside.

2 Place the cornflour in a heatproof bowl that will fit in a steamer and add the crab meat. Mix together gently to coat the crab meat evenly.

3 Place a steamer over a pan of boiling water and put the bowl of crab meat inside it. Cover and steam for 10 minutes and then remove the bowl and set to one side to cool.

4 For the dressing, combine the mustard, vinegar, garlic, pineapple juice, soy sauce, salt and sugar, then stir in 50ml/2fl oz/¼ cup water.

5 Place the pear, cucumber and crab meat in a serving dish and pour over the dressing. Toss the salad and garnish with cress before serving.

Energy 149kcal/630kJ; Protein 10.8g; Carbohydrate 21.2g, of which sugars 17.9g; Fat 2.9g, of which saturates 0.4g; Cholesterol 36mg; Calcium 34mg; Fibre 0.5g; Sodium 812mg.

PASTA, RICE AND NOODLES

Ready-cooked whole lobster or quick-to-cook lobster
tails, crab or prawns are popular all over the world.
For family meals or easy entertaining choose from
simple Italian risottos and pasta dishes, classic
Chinese stir-fries and noodle recipes, or go for the
impressive-looking Lobster Ravioli.

LOBSTER RAVIOLI

This can be made with either fresh cooked or easily available cooked frozen lobster. Defrost frozen lobster overnight in the refrigerator and then simply crack and remove the meat.

SERVES 4 AS A MAIN COURSE,
6 AS AN APPETIZER
450g/1lb cooked lobster meat
2 slices of soft white bread, about
50g/2oz, crusts removed
200ml/7fl oz/scant 1 cup fish stock
1 egg
250ml/8fl oz/1 cup double/heavy cream
15ml/1 tbsp chopped fresh chives
15ml/1 tbsp finely chopped fresh chervil
salt and ground white pepper
fresh chives, to garnish

For the pasta dough
225g/8oz/2 cups strong/hard wheat
    white bread flour
2 eggs, plus 2 egg yolks

For the mushroom sauce
a large pinch of saffron strands
25g/1oz/2 tbsp unsalted butter
2 shallots, finely chopped
200g/7oz/3 cups button/white
    mushrooms, finely chopped
juice of ½ lemon
200ml/7fl oz/scant 1 cup double/heavy
    cream

Energy 652kcal/2722kJ; Protein 23g; Carbohydrate 52.2g, of
which sugars 3.1g; Fat 40.5g, of which saturates 22.2g;
Cholesterol 361mg; Calcium 186mg; Fibre 2.9g; Sodium 298mg.

1 Make the pasta dough. Sift the flour with a pinch of salt. Put into a food processor with the eggs and extra yolks; process until the mixture resembles coarse breadcrumbs. Turn out on to a floured surface and knead to a smooth dough. Wrap in clear film/plastic wrap and rest in the refrigerator for 1 hour.

2 Now make the lobster filling. Cut the lobster meat into small chunks and place in a bowl. Tear the white bread into small pieces and soak in 45ml/3 tbsp fish stock. Place in a food processor with half the egg and 30–45ml/2–3 tbsp of the cream and process until smooth. Stir the mixture into the lobster meat, then add the chives and chervil and season to taste with salt and white pepper.

3 Roll the ravioli dough to a thickness of 3mm/⅛in, preferably using a pasta machine. The process can be done by hand with a rolling pin but is quite hard work. Divide the dough into four long rectangles and dust each rectangle lightly with flour.

4 Spoon 6 equal heaps of filling on to one rectangle of pasta, leaving about 3cm/1¼in between each pile. Lightly beat the remaining egg with a tablespoon of water and brush it over the pasta between the piles of filling. Cover with a second sheet of pasta. Repeat with the other two sheets of pasta and filling.

5 Using your fingertips, press the top layer of dough firmly between the piles of filling, making sure each is well sealed. Cut between the heaps with a 7.5cm/3in fluted pastry cutter, or a pasta wheel, to make 12 ravioli. Place the ravioli in a single layer on a baking sheet, cover with clear film/plastic wrap or a damp cloth, and put in the refrigerator while you make the mushroom sauce.

6 Soak the saffron in 15ml/1 tbsp warm water. Melt the butter in a pan and cook the shallots over a low heat until they are soft but not coloured. Add the chopped mushrooms and lemon juice and continue to cook over a low heat until almost all the liquid has evaporated. Stir in the saffron, with its soaking water, and the cream, then cook gently, stirring occasionally, until the sauce has thickened. Keep warm.

7 In another pan, bring the remaining fish stock to the boil, stir in the rest of the cream and bubble to make a slightly thickened sauce. Season to taste and keep warm. Bring a large pan of lightly salted water to a rolling boil. Gently drop in the ravioli and cook for 3–4 minutes, until the pasta is just tender.

8 Place three ravioli (two for an appetizer) on to the centre of individual warmed plates, spoon over a little of the mushroom sauce and pour a ribbon of fish sauce around the edge. Serve immediately, garnished with chopped and whole fresh chives.

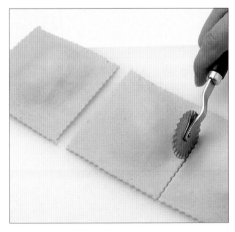

CAPELLI D'ANGELO WITH LOBSTER

SERVES 4
450g/1lb cooked lobster meat
juice of ½ lemon
40g/1½oz/3 tbsp butter
4 fresh tarragon sprigs, leaves stripped
  and chopped
60ml/4 tbsp double/heavy cream
90ml/6 tbsp sparkling dry white wine
60ml/4 tbsp fish stock
300g/11oz fresh capelli d'angelo
salt and ground black pepper
about 10ml/2 tsp lumpfish roe, to
  garnish (optional)

Using ready-cooked lobster makes this an impressive but really easy dish for entertaining friends. Prepare the sauce in advance and then simply cook the pasta just before serving.

1 Cut the lobster meat into small pieces and put it in a bowl. Sprinkle with the lemon juice. Melt the butter in a frying pan, add the lobster meat and tarragon and stir over the heat for a few seconds. Add the cream and stir for a few seconds more, then pour in the wine and stock, with salt and pepper to taste. Simmer gently for 2 minutes, then remove from the heat and cover.

2 Cook the pasta according to the instructions on the packet. Drain well, reserving a few spoonfuls of the cooking water.

3 Place the pan of lobster sauce over a medium to high heat, add the pasta and toss for just long enough to combine and heat through; moisten with a little of the reserved water from the pasta. Serve immediately in warmed bowls, sprinkled with lumpfish roe if you like.

COOK'S TIP
For a midweek family meal, use fresh flat leaf parsley instead of tarragon and dry white wine instead of sparkling wine. Capelli d'Angelo or Angel hair is a very fine pasta. Any other long, thin pasta works well here, try spaghetti, vermicelli or bucatini.

Energy 549kcal/2310kJ; Protein 37g; Carbohydrate 56g, of which sugars 2.9g; Fat 19.6g, of which saturates 10.6g; Cholesterol 179mg; Calcium 108mg; Fibre 2.2g; Sodium 480mg.

TRUFFLE AND LOBSTER RISOTTO

SERVES 4

50g/2oz/4 tbsp unsalted butter
1 medium onion, chopped
350g/12oz/1¾ cups risotto rice,
   preferably carnaroli
1 fresh thyme sprig
150ml/¼ pint/⅔ cup dry white wine
1.2 litres/2 pints/5 cups simmering fish
   stock
450g/1lb cooked lobster meat
45ml/3 tbsp chopped mixed fresh
   parsley and chervil
3–4 drops truffle oil
2 hard-boiled eggs
1 fresh black or white truffle
salt and ground black pepper

Energy 520kcal/2172kJ; Protein 19.9g; Carbohydrate 71.3g, of
which sugars 1.2g; Fat 14.3g, of which saturates 7.4g;
Cholesterol 172mg; Calcium 68mg; Fibre 0.2g; Sodium 263mg.

Truffle shavings and truffle oil are added towards the end of the cooking to preserve their unique flavour. A frozen, defrosted cooked lobster works equally as well as a fresh one.

1 Melt the butter in a large pan, add the onion and fry until softened but not browned. Add the rice and stir well to coat with the butter. Cook until the rice is slightly translucent. Add the thyme, then the wine, and cook until it has been absorbed. Add the hot fish stock a little at a time, stirring. Let each ladleful be absorbed before adding the next.

2 Cut half the extracted lobster meat into large chunks, then roughly chop the remainder.

3 When the rice is tender and the last ladle of stock has been absorbed, stir the roughly chopped lobster meat, half the chopped herbs, and the truffle oil into the risotto. Remove from the heat, cover, and leave to stand for 5 minutes to allow the flavours to permeate.

4 Divide among four warmed plates and place the lobster chunks on top in the centre of the risotto. Cut the hard-boiled eggs into wedges and arrange them around the lobster meat. Finally, shave a little fresh truffle over each portion and sprinkle with the remaining herbs. Serve immediately.

LOBSTER NOODLES

Egg noodles are stir-fried with garlic, beansprouts, oyster sauce and freshly cooked lobster meat. If you want to decorate the finished dish with the lobster shell, be very careful when removing the meat, so that the whole shell stays intact.

SERVES 4
1 large live lobster, about 1kg/2¼lb
400g/14oz dried egg noodles
30ml/2 tbsp vegetable oil
15ml/1 tbsp crushed garlic
115g/4oz/1 cup beansprouts
200ml/7fl oz/scant 1 cup water
30ml/2 tbsp oyster sauce
5ml/1 tsp ground black pepper
30ml/2 tbsp sesame oil

COOK'S TIP
Shellfish is a popular choice in Chinese cuisine – this typical lobster dish is often made with warm water rock or spiny lobster rather than cold water American or European lobster. As an easy alternative to whole live lobster, this can also be made as a quick supper by adding steamed lobster tails (see page 29) to the noodles.

1 To prepare the lobster, follow the instructions on page 19 and cook for 10 minutes or until the shell has turned scarlet. Remove the lobster from the water and set aside to cool.

2 Heat a separate pan of water and cook the noodles according to the instructions on the packet. Drain and set aside.

3 When the lobster is cool enough to handle, use a sharp knife to cut off the head and the tip of the tail. Rinse and set aside for the garnish. Twist off the claws and set aside.

4 Using a sharp pair of poultry shears or strong scissors, cut down the shell from the top to the tail. Remove the lobster meat, and using a sharp knife remove the dark thread that runs along the length of the tail and discard. Slice the meat into rounds. Remove the meat from the claws and legs. Set all the lobster meat aside and reserve the shell to garnish the dish.

5 Heat the oil in a wok and fry the garlic for 40 seconds. Add the beansprouts and toss over the heat for 2 minutes. Add the noodles, 200ml/7fl oz/scant 1 cup water, oyster sauce, black pepper and sesame oil and cook, stirring, for 2 minutes.

6 Add the lobster slices and toss lightly. Arrange on a large plate, making sure that the lobster pieces are fairly prominent. Decorate with the lobster head and tail and serve.

Energy 501kcal/2110kJ; Protein 29.9g; Carbohydrate 56.9g, of which sugars 4g; Fat 18.8g, of which saturates 3.5g; Cholesterol 123mg; Calcium 83mg; Fibre 2.6g; Sodium 559mg.

STEAMED LANGOUSTINES WITH LEMON GRASS RISOTTO

SERVES 4

8 raw langoustines
30ml/2 tbsp olive oil
15ml/1 tbsp unsalted butter
1 onion, finely chopped
1 carrot, finely diced
1 celery stick, finely diced
30ml/2 tbsp very finely chopped lemon
　grass
300g/11oz/1½ cups arborio rice
200ml/7fl oz/scant 1 cup dry white wine
1.5 litres/2½ pints/6¼ cups simmering
　vegetable stock
50ml/2fl oz/¼ cup Thai fish sauce
　(nam pla)
30ml/2 tbsp finely chopped
　Chinese chives
salt and ground black pepper

Traditional Italian risotto is given a subtle Asian twist with the addition of fragrant lemon grass, Thai fish sauce and Chinese chives. The delicate citrus-flavoured rice is the perfect partner for simple steamed langoustines. If you cannot find fresh langoustines (also known as Dublin Bay prawns) you can use king prawns/jumbo shrimp in their shells instead.

1 Place the langoustines in a baking parchment-lined bamboo steamer, cover and place over a wok of simmering water. Steam for 6–8 minutes, remove from the heat and keep warm.

2 Heat the oil and butter in a wok and add the vegetables. Cook over a high heat for 2–3 minutes. Add the lemon grass and rice and stir-fry for 2 minutes.

3 Add the wine to the wok, reduce the heat and slowly stir until the wine is absorbed. Add about 250ml/8fl oz/1 cup of the stock and cook gently, stirring until absorbed.

4 Continue adding the stock, about 120ml/4fl oz/½ cup at a time, stirring until fully absorbed before adding more. Cook until the rice is just tender.

5 Stir the fish sauce and the Chinese chives into the risotto, check the seasoning and serve on warmed plates. Top each serving with 2 langoustines.

Energy 430kcal/1811kJ; Protein 12g; Carbohydrate 72g, of which sugars 4g; Fat 12g, of which saturates 3g; Cholesterol 66mg; Calcium 54mg; Fibre 3g; Sodium 1207mg.

OVEN-BAKED LOBSTER AND SPINACH RISOTTO

If you'd rather not stand at the hob stirring a pan of risotto, this is an alternative method to get the same delicious results. For a really simple dish stir in cooked king prawns just before serving instead of the lobster.

SERVES 4

2 lemon slices
2 sprigs of fresh flat leaf parsley
2 sprigs of fresh dill
4 raw lobster tails, shell on
40g/1½oz/3 tbsp unsalted butter
15ml/1 tbsp olive oil
1 onion, finely chopped
2 garlic cloves, finely chopped
300g/11oz/1½ cups risotto rice
400ml/14fl oz/1⅔ cups fish stock
175ml/6fl oz/¾ cup dry white wine
100g/3¾oz baby spinach
40g/1½oz/1½ cups Parmesan cheese, grated plus extra shavings, to serve
60ml/4 tbsp chopped fresh flat leaf parsley
salt and ground black pepper

1 Pour 300ml/½ pint/1¼ cups water into a medium pan and add the lemon, parsley and dill. Bring the water to the boil and then add the lobster tails, shell side down. Reduce the heat, cover and simmer gently for 8–10 minutes or until the flesh is firm and opaque. The lobster shells will turn a dark red colour.

2 Using a slotted spoon, remove the tails from the pan and reserve the cooking liquid. Place the tails shell side down on a plate and, using sharp kitchen scissors or poultry shears, cut through the underside of the body and gently pull the shell away. Using a sharp knife remove and discard the dark black thread that runs along the length of the tail. Chop the meat into bite-sized pieces.

3 Strain the reserved stock and set aside. Preheat the oven to 200°C/400°F/Gas 6.

4 In an ovenproof casserole dish, add the butter, olive oil, onion and garlic and sauté gently for 5 minutes. Add the rice and stir well to coat in the butter and oil. Pour in the reserved stock together with the fish stock and wine. Increase the heat and bring to the boil.

5 Season well and cover with a tight-fitting lid. Transfer to the oven and bake for 20–25 minutes, until the rice is tender, stirring occasionally during cooking.

6 Remove the cooked risotto from the oven and stir in the spinach, cheese and parsley. Finally, stir in the chopped lobster and serve immediately dotted with Parmesan shavings.

Energy 472kcal/1969kJ; Protein 15.4g; Carbohydrate 61g, of which sugars 1.1g; Fat 15.1g, of which saturates 7.6g; Cholesterol 56mg; Calcium 204mg; Fibre 1.5g; Sodium 252mg.

LINGUINE WITH CRAB

SERVES 4

250g/9oz cooked white or mixed white
   and brown crab meat
45ml/3 tbsp olive oil
1 small handful of fresh flat leaf
   parsley, roughly chopped, plus extra
   to garnish
1 garlic clove, crushed
350g/12oz ripe Italian plum tomatoes,
   skinned and chopped
60–90ml/4–6 tbsp dry white wine
350g/12oz fresh or dried linguine
salt and ground black pepper

Choose either all white crab meat or a half and half
mixture of brown and white for this classic pasta dish.
White crab meat has a sweet, delicate flavour and a
flaky texture, whereas brown meat is richer, has a
more concentrated flavour and a creamier texture.

1 Put the crab meat in a mortar and pound to a rough pulp with a pestle. If you
do not have a mortar and pestle, use a sturdy bowl and the end of a rolling pin.
Set aside.

2 Heat 30ml/2 tbsp of the oil in a large pan. Add the parsley and garlic, with salt
and pepper to taste, and fry for a few minutes until the garlic begins to brown.

3 Add the tomatoes, pounded crab meat and wine, cover the pan and simmer
gently for 15 minutes, stirring occasionally.

4 Meanwhile, cook the pasta according to the instructions on the packet,
draining it the moment it is al dente, and reserving a little of the cooking water.

5 Return the pasta to the clean pan, add the remaining oil and toss quickly over
a medium heat until the oil coats the strands.

6 Add the tomato and crab mixture to the pasta and toss again, adding a little
of the reserved cooking water if you think it necessary. Adjust the seasoning to
taste. Serve hot, in warmed bowls, sprinkled with parsley.

Energy 457kcal/1932kJ; Protein 22.8g; Carbohydrate 68g, of which sugars 6g; Fat 10.8g, of which saturates 1.5g; Cholesterol 45mg;
Calcium 125mg; Fibre 3.9g; Sodium 359mg.

CRAB WITH MUSHROOMS AND NOODLES

This is a delicious crab dish that contains a wonderful mix of textures and flavours. The recipe takes just minutes to cook, so make sure you have all the ingredients completely prepared before you begin, and serve as soon as it's ready.

SERVES 4

25g/1oz dried cloud ear/wood ear
  mushrooms
115g/4oz dried bean thread/
  cellophane noodles
30ml/2 tbsp vegetable or sesame oil
3 shallots, halved and thinly sliced
2 garlic cloves, crushed
2 green or red chillies, seeded and sliced
1 carrot, sliced
5ml/1 tsp sugar
45ml/3 tbsp oyster sauce
15ml/1 tbsp soy sauce
400ml/14fl oz/1⅔ cups fish stock
225g/8oz cooked white crab meat, cut
  into bitesize chunks
ground black pepper
fresh coriander/cilantro leaves,
  to garnish

1 Soak the mushrooms and noodles in warm water, in separate bowls, for 15 minutes. Remove the centres from the soaked cloud ear mushrooms and cut the mushrooms in half. Drain the soaked noodles and cut into pieces.

2 Heat a wok or heavy pan and add 15ml/1 tbsp of the oil. Stir in the shallots, garlic and chillies, and cook until fragrant. Add the carrot slices and cook for 1 minute, then add the mushrooms. Stir in the sugar with the oyster and soy sauces, followed by the bean thread noodles.

3 Pour in the stock, cover the wok or pan and cook for 5 minutes, or until the noodles are soft and have absorbed most of the sauce.

4 Meanwhile, heat the remaining oil in a heavy pan. Add the crab meat and cook until it is hot and tender. Season well with black pepper. Divide the noodles, vegetables, sauce and crab meat into warmed serving bowls, and serve garnished with coriander.

Energy 292Kcal/1224kJ; Protein 16g; Carbohydrate 30g, of which sugars 5g; Fat 13g, of which saturates 2g; Cholesterol 36mg; Calcium 29mg; Fibre 2.5g; Sodium 1g.

STIR-FRIED PRAWNS WITH RICE NOODLES

One of the most appealing aspects of Asian food is that ingredients are carefully chosen so each dish is balanced. Here the classic combination of juicy prawns and delicate rice noodles complement each other.

SERVES 4
115g/4oz rice noodles
75g/30z mooli/daikon
150g/5oz large prawns/shrimp, with shells
30ml/2 tbsp groundnut/peanut oil
1 large garlic clove, crushed
15g/½oz dried shrimps
15ml/1 tbsp Thai fish sauce (nam pla)
30ml/2 tbsp soy sauce
30ml/2 tbsp light muscovado/brown sugar
30ml/2 tbsp lime juice
115g/4oz/1 cup beansprouts
50g/2oz/½ cup peanuts, chopped
15ml/1 tbsp sesame oil
chopped fresh coriander/cilantro, 5ml/1 tsp dried chilli flakes and 2 shallots, finely chopped, to garnish

1 Soak the noodles in a bowl of boiling water for 5 minutes, or according to the packet instructions. Grate the mooli. Peel and devein the prawns: make a shallow cut down the back of each prawn, and, using the tip of the knife, pull out and discard the intestinal tract.

2 Heat the oil in a wok or large frying pan. Add the garlic, and stir-fry over medium heat for 2–3 minutes, until golden brown. Add the grated mooli and prawns along with the dried shrimps and stir-fry for a further 2 minutes. Stir in the fish sauce, soy sauce, sugar and lime juice.

3 Drain the noodles thoroughly, then snip them into smaller lengths with scissors. Add to the wok or pan with the beansprouts, peanuts and sesame oil. Toss to mix, then stir-fry for 2 minutes. Serve immediately, garnished with the coriander, chilli flakes and shallots.

COOK'S TIP
Some cooks salt the mooli and leave it to drain, then rinse and dry before use.

Energy 397kcal/1675kJ; Protein 21.3g; Carbohydrate 56.5g, of which sugars 3.2g; Fat 11.1g, of which saturates 2.4g; Cholesterol 89mg; Calcium 72mg; Fibre 3.3g; Sodium 567mg.

FIRES AND GRILLS

Lobster, prawns and crawfish are all well suited to
very hot, quick cooking. Classic Lobster Thermidor
or Grilled Lobster with Tarragon Cream are great
dinner party dishes. Prawns are always a barbecue
favourite; here chilli, limes, lemon grass or satay
sauce enhance their sweet flavour.

GRILLED LOBSTER WITH TARRAGON CREAM

Lobsters are at their best prepared simply to make the most of their firm, sweet meat. Fresh herbs, cream and melted butter are used here to enhance their natural flavour. This recipe can be also be made with ready-cooked lobsters – either fresh or frozen. If using frozen cooked lobster, allow it to thaw out thoroughly in the refrigerator before using.

SERVES 4
2 live lobsters, 675–800g/1½–1¾lb each
grated rind of 1 orange
75g/3oz/6 tbsp unsalted butter
50ml/2fl oz/¼ cup whipping cream
2 sprigs of fresh tarragon, plus extra to
   garnish
salt and cayenne pepper

1 Prepare the live lobsters following the instructions on page 19, and cook in a large pan of water together with the grated orange rind for about 5 minutes.

2 Drain the lobsters, retaining the stock if you wish, and once cool enough to handle, split the lobsters in two down the middle with a sharp knife. Remove the stomach sac from the head and the intestine tract, which runs down the tail. Remove and crack open the claws. Remove the meat and place it in the head.

3 Melt the butter and brush it liberally over the four half lobsters, covering all the exposed flesh. Season lightly with salt and a little cayenne pepper.

4 Preheat the grill or broiler to high. Pour the cream into a pan over a low heat and add the sprigs of tarragon, stirring it in gently. Bring the cream to just below boiling point, turn the heat right down and infuse the flavours for 10 minutes.

5 Put the lobsters under the preheated grill for about 7–10 minutes and then remove from the grill. Pour the buttery lobster juices from the grill pan into the cream and turn the heat up a fraction. Bring the cream mixture to the boil, whisking to combine. Strain the sauce.

6 Place half a lobster on each warmed serving plate, and gently spoon over the cream sauce, letting it spill over on to the plate. Serve immediately garnished with tarragon sprigs.

VARIATION
Lobster also works well with other fresh herbs; try a few sprigs of wild garlic or fresh dill for an equally lovely flavour.

Energy 284kcal/1180kJ; Protein 20.8g; Carbohydrate 0.8g, of which sugars 0.8g; Fat 22.1g, of which saturates 13.2g; Cholesterol 153mg; Calcium 91mg; Fibre 0.6g; Sodium 421mg.

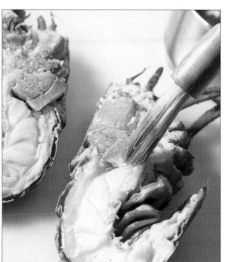

SPICED LOBSTER IN BANANA LEAF

SERVES 4

2 raw lobster tails, shelled and coarsely minced/ground
2 eggs, lightly beaten
30ml/2 tbsp vegetable oil
175ml/6fl oz/¾ cup coconut cream
8 pieces banana leaf, each measuring 25cm/10in square
lime wedges, to serve

For the spice paste
200g/7oz onion, chopped
6 candlenuts
15ml/1 tbsp ground coriander
10ml/2 tsp chilli powder
15g/½oz galangal, peeled and chopped
5ml/1 tsp ground turmeric
15g/½oz shrimp paste
4 lime leaves, cut into fine ribbons
5ml/1 tsp salt
5ml/1 tsp sugar

COOK'S TIP

To shell a lobster tail insert kitchen shears between the shell and the meat. Cut down the centre of the shell leaving the fan tail attached. Gently loosen and lift the meat out of the shell.

Any food that is spiced and wrapped in banana leaf before being cooked is known as otak otak in Malaysia and Singapore. This decadent version of the recipe uses lobster for a spectacular and delicious party piece, but you could use the same method to cook any firm fish. Banana leaves are available to buy online.

1 To make the spice paste, grind the onion, candlenuts, spices and shrimp paste together until fine, using a mortar and pestle or a food processor. Mix with the lime leaves, salt and sugar and transfer to a bowl.

2 Add the minced lobster to the bowl and mix well with the spices. Add the eggs, oil and coconut cream and stir thoroughly. The consistency should be like that of softened butter.

3 Scald the banana leaves in boiling water to soften them, and drain. Lay each piece of leaf out on a flat surface and place 30–45ml/2–3 tbsp of the spiced lobster mixture in the centre, spreading it out until it is about 5mm/¼in thick.

4 Fold the opposite edges of the leaf over the filling and tuck in the sides to make a firm parcel.

5 Prepare a charcoal grill or preheat a grill or broiler to high. Grill the banana leaf parcels for 8–10 minutes, turning once halfway through cooking. Serve immediately with lime wedges, to be unwrapped at the table.

Energy 369Kcal/1531kJ; Protein 18.5g; Carbohydrate 8g, of which sugars 4.6g; Fat 29.7g, of which saturates 16.5g; Cholesterol 168mg; Calcium 119mg; Fibre 0.8g; Sodium 359mg.

LOBSTER THERMIDOR

Probably the most well-known lobster recipe of all – sweet lobster meat
is combined with a creamy brandy-flavoured béchamel sauce, popped back
in the shell and then grilled until golden. For extra flavour the classic recipe
includes the coral and liver in the sauce, but this is optional.

SERVES 2–4
2 live lobsters, about 675g/1½lb each
20g/¾oz/1½ tbsp unsalted butter
30ml/2 tbsp plain/all-purpose flour
30ml/2 tbsp brandy
120ml/4fl oz/½ cup milk
90ml/6 tbsp whipping cream
15ml/1 tbsp Dijon mustard
lemon juice, to taste
salt and white pepper
grated Parmesan cheese, for sprinkling
fresh parsley and dill, to garnish

1 Prepare and cook the lobsters for 8–10 minutes following the instructions on page 19. Once cool enough to handle, split the lobsters in two down the middle with a sharp knife. Remove the stomach sac from the head and the intestine tract, which runs down the tail. Remove the meat from the shells, reserving the coral and liver, then rinse the shells and wipe dry. Cut the meat into bite-size pieces.

2 Melt the butter in a heavy pan over a medium-high heat. Stir in the flour and cook, stirring, until slightly golden. Pour in the brandy and milk, whisking vigorously until smooth, then whisk in the cream and mustard.

3 If using, push the lobster coral and liver through a sieve or strainer into the sauce and whisk to blend. Reduce the heat to low and simmer gently for about 10 minutes, stirring often, until thickened. Season with salt, if needed, white pepper and lemon juice.

4 Preheat the grill or broiler. Arrange the lobster shells in a gratin dish or shallow, flameproof baking dish.

5 Stir the lobster meat into the sauce and divide the mixture evenly among the shells. Sprinkle lightly with Parmesan and grill or broil for a few minutes until golden and bubbling. Serve garnished with herbs.

Energy 859kcal/3573kJ; Protein 56g; Carbohydrate 9.8g, of which sugars 2g; Fat 59.6g, of which saturates 33.8g; Cholesterol 536mg; Calcium 488mg; Fibre 1.2g; Sodium 976mg.

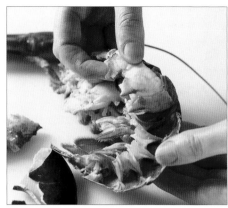

LOBSTER WITH WHOLEGRAIN MUSTARD AND CREAM

SERVES 2
1 live lobster, about 500g/1¼lb
10ml/2 tsp unsalted butter, plus
  50g/2oz/¼ cup unsalted butter,
  melted
splash of whisky (grain not malt)
1 shallot or ½ onion, finely chopped
50g/2oz button/white mushrooms
splash of white wine
175ml/6fl oz/¾ cup double/heavy
  cream
5ml/1 tsp wholegrain mustard
10ml/2 tsp chopped fresh chervil
5ml/1 tsp tarragon
60ml/4 tbsp breadcrumbs
salt and ground black pepper

COOK'S TIP
This can also be served as a starter–
divide the lobster mixture between 4
ramekins and top with the breadcrumbs
and butter and grill or broil until
cooked through and browned.

Succulent lobster with a rich and decadent sauce flavoured with mushrooms, shallot, fresh chervil and tarragon needs nothing more than a simple salad and crusty bread as an accompaniment. Precooked lobster can be used as an alternative to cooking a whole lobster, if preferred.

1 Prepare and cook the lobster for 8–10 minutes following the instructions on page 19. Once cool enough to handle, split the lobster in two down the middle with a sharp knife. Remove the stomach sac from the head and the intestine tract, which runs down the tail. Remove the meat from the tail, taking care to keep it intact.

2 Cut the tail meat into slanted slices. Remove the meat from the claws, keeping it as whole as possible. Wash the two half-shells out and set aside.

3 Heat a frying pan over a low heat, add the butter and wait for it to bubble. Gently add the lobster meat and colour lightly (don't overcook or it will dry out). Pour in the whisky, stir well and then remove the lobster meat.

4 Add the chopped shallot or onion and the mushrooms, and cook gently over a medium-low heat for a few minutes until soft and the onion or shallot is transparent. Add a little white wine, then the cream, and allow to simmer to reduce to a light coating texture. Then add the mustard and the chopped herbs and mix well. Season to taste with a little salt and freshly ground black pepper. Meanwhile preheat the grill or broiler to high.

5 Place the two lobster half-shells on the grill pan. Distribute the lobster meat evenly throughout the two half-shells and spoon the sauce over. Sprinkle with breadcrumbs, drizzle with melted butter and brown under the preheated grill. Serve immediately.

Energy 812kcal/3357kJ; Protein 23.6g; Carbohydrate 12g, of which sugars 3.7g; Fat 74.9g, of which saturates 46g; Cholesterol 287mg; Calcium 127mg; Fibre 0.9g; Sodium 580mg.

PERI-PERI CRAYFISH

These small spiny lobsters are a real delicacy, especially when cooked on a barbecue. If you can't get find crayfish, lobster works just as well. The sauce is a hot and fiery sauce from Portugal, traditionally made using peri-peri, a variety of African bird's eye chilli. Here it's made with chilli-flavoured oil plus fresh parsley and marjoram, lemon juice and garlic.

SERVES 4–6

2 x 350–500g/12oz–1¼lb live crayfish or
   1 x 800g/1¾lb lobster
40g/1½oz/3 tbsp unsalted butter,
   melted
salt, cayenne and black pepper
a little melted unsalted butter and
   lemon wedges, to serve

For the peri-peri sauce

30ml/2 tbsp vegetable oil
3 garlic cloves, peeled and sliced into
   thin slivers
1 red, 1 yellow, and 1 green/bell
   pepper, seeded and finely chopped
100ml/3½fl oz/scant ½ cup peri-peri
   chilli oil
30ml/2 tbsp finely chopped fresh
   parsley
5ml/1 tsp finely chopped fresh
   marjoram
juice of 1 lemon

COOK'S TIP

The tomalley serves as the crayfish's liver and pancreas and is found in the head. Many consider it a delicacy, and eat it as it is; it is also often used to flavour sauces and stocks. However, it is the organ that filters waste, and there is a possibility it could be contaminated with pollutants, so it must be cooked properly.

1 Place the crayfish in the freezer for a couple of hours before cooking, as this makes them easier to process. Preheat the grill, broiler or barbecue. When the flames have died down, the coals are ready.

2 Remove the crayfish from the freezer and place on a wooden board. Push the tip of a heavy sharp blade through the back of the head, then cut the whole crayfish in half lengthways.

3 Brush the flesh of the crayfish with the melted butter and season with a pinch of cayenne pepper and a little salt and black pepper.

4 To make the peri-peri sauce, heat the vegetable oil in a medium-sized frying pan, add the garlic and cook for 1 minute stirring well. Add the chopped peppers and cook for 1 minute. Add the peri-peri oil and remove from the heat. Stir in the herbs and lemon juice and season with a little salt and cayenne pepper, to taste. Set aside.

5 When the fire is ready place the crayfish shell side down on the grill and cook for 5 minutes until the flesh is firm but still slightly opaque. Check the tomalley is firm and cooked right through. Transfer to a serving plate.

6 To serve, spoon a little melted butter over the flesh of the crayfish, add a squeeze of lemon and liberally drizzle the peri-peri sauce on the tail and into the tomalley in the head.

COOK'S TIP

As crayfish are not too fussy about what they eat it is best to purge them for 24 hours before cooking. Follow the instructions on page 23.

Energy 259kcal/1072kJ; Protein 8.8g; Carbohydrate 7.1g, of which sugars 6.2g; Fat 21.9g, of which saturates 5.8g; Cholesterol 53mg; Calcium 43mg; Fibre 2.6g; Sodium 162mg.

GRILLED LOBSTER WITH BASIL MAYONNAISE

This is a smart yet unpretentious dish that is well worth the effort. The mayo is flavoured with home-made basil oil, which needs to be made in advance and left to infuse overnight. For a quicker version, look for basil-infused oil in the supermarket or use a ready-made lemon-infused olive oil.

1 To make the basil oil, place the basil leaves in a bowl and pour boiling water over them. Leave for about 30 seconds until the leaves turn a brighter green. Drain, refresh under cold running water, drain again, then squeeze dry in kitchen paper. Place in a food processor. Add both oils and process to a purée. Scrape into a bowl, cover and chill overnight.

2 Place the lobsters in the freezer for a couple of hours before cooking, as this makes them easier to process. Preheat the grill or broiler or barbecue. When the flames have died down the coals are ready.

3 Line a sieve with muslin or cheesecloth and set it over a deep bowl. Pour in the basil and oil purée and leave undisturbed for about 1 hour, or until all the oil has filtered through into the bowl. The solids left behind in the sieve can now be discarded. Cover well and chill the basil oil until needed.

4 Make the mayonnaise. Place the crushed garlic in a bowl. Add the mustard with 2.5ml/½ tsp of the lemon juice and seasoning. Mix well. Whisk in the egg yolks, then add the basil oil, a drop at a time, whisking continuously until the mixture starts to thicken. Now start adding the oil a little faster. When you have about 45ml/3 tbsp oil left, whisk in the remaining lemon juice and the rest of the oil. Finally, whisk in 7.5ml/1½ tsp cold water. Cover and chill until needed.

5 Remove the lobsters from the freezer and place on a wooden board. Push the tip of a heavy sharp blade through the back of the heads, then cut each whole lobster in half lengthways.

6 Prepare the barbecue. Chop the basil and mix it with the olive oil and garlic in a bowl. Season lightly. Position a lightly oiled grill rack over the coals.

7 When the coals are ready, brush some of the oil mixture over the cut side of each lobster half. Place cut-side down on the grill. Grill the lobster for 5 minutes then turn over, baste with more oil mixture and cook for 10–15 minutes more, basting and moving about the rack occasionally. Grill the lime halves at the same time, placing them cut-side down for 3 minutes. This helps to release their juices and gives a slight caramel flavour.

8 Serve the lobster straight from the grill with the basil mayonnaise for dipping and the grilled lime halves for squeezing.

SERVES 4
2 live lobsters, about 675g/1½lb each
15 fresh basil leaves, roughly chopped
60ml/4 tbsp olive oil
1 garlic clove, crushed
salt and ground black pepper
2 limes, halved, to serve

For the basil oil and mayonnaise
40g/1½oz/1½ cups basil leaves stripped
    from their stalks
200ml/7fl oz/1 cup sunflower oil, plus
    extra if needed
45ml/3 tbsp olive oil
1 small garlic clove, crushed
2.5ml/½ tsp dry English/hot mustard
10ml/2 tsp lemon juice
2 egg yolks
ground white pepper

Energy 618kcal/2555kJ; Protein 22g; Carbohydrate 1g, of which sugars 0.1g; Fat 58.6g, of which saturates 8g; Cholesterol 201mg; Calcium 99mg; Fibre 0.1g; Sodium 324mg.

This mildly spiced seafood dish is perfect for enjoying during the summer and can be cooked on a griddle pan or barbecue. The vegetables add a beautiful decorative touch to the presentation.

GRIDDLED TIGER PRAWNS

SERVES 2

6 raw tiger prawns/jumbo shrimp
6 wooden skewers, soaked in water for
 30 minutes
15ml/1 tbsp white wine
15ml/1 tbsp sake
2.5ml/½ tsp chilli oil
7.5ml/1½ tsp sesame oil
1 garlic clove, finely sliced
½ green chilli, seeded and sliced
½ red chilli, seeded and sliced
½ shiitake mushroom, finely sliced
30ml/2 tbsp dark soy sauce
lemon juice, to taste
salt and ground black pepper
finely pared lemon rind, to garnish

1 Remove the head and shell from the prawns, leaving the tail intact. Make a shallow cut down the back of each prawn. Using the tip of the knife, pull out and discard the dark intestinal tract. Rinse in cold water and dry gently with kitchen paper.

2 Thread each prawn on to a skewer, piercing first through the tail and then through the head.

3 Score the skewered prawns on both sides and then place them in a bowl. Add the wine, sake and chilli oil. Season with salt and pepper, then toss the prawns to coat them evenly in the marinade and set aside for 15 minutes. Light the barbecue, if using.

4 Meanwhile heat a wok over medium heat and add the sesame oil. One ingredient at a time, stir-fry the garlic, chillies and shiitake mushroom, keeping them separate. Season with a pinch of salt and set aside.

5 When the coals are ready, place an oiled grill rack on top and cook the prawns for about 5 minutes, brushing them with soy sauce and turning once to prevent them from burning. Or heat a griddle pan and cook the same way.

6 Arrange three skewers on each plate. Add a little of the stir-fried vegetables and a squeeze of lemon juice. Garnish with a little lemon rind and serve.

Per portion Energy 142kcal/593kJ; Protein 13.4g; Carbohydrate 9g, of which sugars 8.7g; Fat 6g, of which saturates 0.7g; Cholesterol 146mg; Calcium 67mg; Fibre 0.2g; Sodium 144mg.

BARBECUED KING PRAWNS

These huge prawns can grow up to 33cm/13in in length, and are great for grilling on a barbecue. This dish is fast and easy, yet impressive; ideal for a relaxed poolside lunch with salad or for serving as an appetizer while the main course is cooking.

SERVES 6

6 raw giant Mediterranean prawns/
   extra large jumbo shrimp, total
   weight about 900g/2lb
juice of 2 limes
60ml/4 tbsp olive oil
12 large kaffir lime leaves
12 pandanus leaves
6 wooden cocktail sticks/toothpicks,
   soaked in water for 30 minutes
mayonnaise, to serve
2 limes cut into wedges, to serve

1 Make a shallow cut down the curved back of each prawn and place them in a shallow dish.

2 In a separate bowl, mix the lime juice and oil together and then pour the mixture over the prawns. Set the prawns aside for 15 minutes to marinate. Meanwhile prepare the barbecue.

3 Take each prawn, lay two kaffir lime leaves on top, wrap two pandanus leaves around it and skewer with a cocktail stick.

4 Once the flames have died down, position a lightly oiled grill rack over the coals to heat. When the coals are medium-hot, grill the wrapped prawns for 3 minutes on each side. Serve with mayonnaise and lime wedges. To eat, unwrap the prawns, peel off the shell and remove the black vein with your fingers.

Energy 72kcal/306kJ; Protein 12.9g; Carbohydrate 0g, of which sugars 0g; Fat 2.3g, of which saturates 0.4g; Cholesterol 158mg; Calcium 65mg; Fibre 0g; Sodium 900mg.

SATAY PRAWNS

This delicious dish is similar to the Indonesian satay. The combination of mild peanuts, aromatic spices, sweet coconut milk and zesty lemon juice in the spicy dip is a wonderful accompaniment to king prawns.

SERVES 4–6

450g/1lb raw king prawns/jumbo shrimp, peeled and deveined

12 wooden skewers, soaked in water for 30 minutes

25ml/1½ tbsp vegetable oil

spring onions/scallions, to serve

For the satay sauce

25ml/1½ tbsp vegetable oil

15ml/1 tbsp chopped garlic

1 small onion, chopped

15ml/1 tbsp tamarind paste

3 fresh red chillies, seeded and chopped

3 kaffir lime leaves, torn

1 lemon grass stalk, finely chopped

5ml/1 tsp medium curry paste

250ml/8fl oz/1 cup coconut milk

1cm/½in piece cinnamon stick

75g/3oz/⅓ cup crunchy peanut butter

30ml/2 tbsp Thai fish sauce (nam pla)

30ml/2 tbsp muscovado/brown sugar

juice of ½ lemon

Energy 219kcal/913kJ; Protein 16.6g; Carbohydrate 10.1g, of which sugars 9g; Fat 12.7g, of which saturates 2.4g; Cholesterol 146mg; Calcium 98mg; Fibre 1.2g; Sodium 414mg.

1 Make the satay sauce. Heat half the oil in a wok or large, heavy frying pan. Add the garlic and onion and cook over a medium heat, stirring occasionally, for 3–4 minutes, until the mixture has softened but not browned. Mix the tamarind paste with 30ml/2 tbsp warm water.

2 Add the chillies, kaffir lime leaves, lemon grass and curry paste. Stir well and cook for a further 2–3 minutes, then stir in the coconut milk, cinnamon stick, peanut butter, fish sauce, sugar and lemon juice. Cook, stirring constantly, until well blended.

3 Bring to the boil, then reduce the heat to low and simmer gently for 15–20 minutes, until the sauce thickens. Stir occasionally with a wooden spoon to prevent the sauce from sticking to the base of the wok or frying pan. Remove the cinnamon stick from the sauce and discard.

4 Preheat the grill or broiler. Thread the prawns on to skewers and brush with a little oil. Cook under the grill for 2 minutes on each side until they turn pink and are firm to the touch. Arrange the skewered prawns on a warmed platter, garnish with shredded spring onions, and serve with the sauce.

PRAWNS **WITH LEMON GRASS**

This is an Indo-Chinese inspired dish – the use of lemon grass is a classic feature of this cuisine. Perfect as an appetizer on a beach barbecue as they cook so rapidly, and can be transported in their marinade.

SERVES 4

16 raw king prawns/jumbo shrimp, cleaned, with shells intact
120ml/4fl oz/½ cup Thai fish sauce (nam pla)
30ml/2 tbsp sugar
15ml/1 tbsp vegetable or sesame oil
3 lemon grass stalks, trimmed and finely chopped

COOK'S TIP
Lemon grass adds a fresh subtle tangy citrus flavour to the prawns, without overpowering their sweet succulent taste. As an alternative use ½ tsp finely grated lemon rind in place of each stalk.

Nutritional information per portion: Energy 174Kcal/726kJ; Protein 13g; Carbohydrate 11g, of which sugars 0g; Fat 9g, of which saturates 1g; Cholesterol 169mg; Calcium 30mg; Fibre 0.3g; Sodium 0.3g.

1 Using a small sharp knife, carefully slice open each king prawn shell along the back and pull out the black vein, using the point of the knife. Try to keep the rest of the shell intact. Place the deveined prawns in a shallow dish.

2 Put the fish sauce in a small bowl with the sugar, and beat together until the sugar has dissolved completely. Add the oil and lemon grass and mix well.

3 Pour the marinade over the prawns, using your fingers to rub it all over the prawns and inside the shells too. Cover the dish with clear film/plastic wrap and chill for at least 4 hours.

4 Light the barbecue or preheat the grill or broiler. When the coals are ready, place an oiled grill rack on top and cook the prawns for 2–3 minutes each side. Serve with little bowls of water for rinsing sticky fingers.

BAKES, STEWS AND STEAMED DISHES

Different types of seafood often work well together.
When a wide selection is readily available —
either the best of the day's catch or at the
fishmonger — combine lobster and squid to make a
hearty casserole, steam lobster and crab together,
or try a creamy bake with prawns and scallops.

SARDINIAN FISH STEW WITH LOBSTER

This is a traditional recipe from the Italian island of Sardinia. Like all good seafood stews it relies on a wide selection of different kinds of fish and seafood, and a few very simple ingredients turn it into a memorable gastronomic experience. It is served with crispy toasted garlic and chilli croutes to mop up all the delicious rich tomato sauce.

1 Before cooking, place the lobster in the freezer for a couple of hours to render it unconscious. Kill the lobster following the instructions on page 19.

2 Heat the oil in a large pan, add the onion, the chopped garlic clove and the parsley, and fry for 5 minutes, until softened but not browned. Add the tomatoes, a pinch of salt and the chopped chilli. Simmer for about 10 minutes, stirring gently.

3 Add the chunks of fish, starting with the thickest pieces and ending with the whole lobster, basting with the sauce as you add each type of fish. Add 200ml/7fl oz/scant 1 cup boiling water to the pan, cover and simmer over the lowest heat for about 1 hour.

4 Rub the slices of bread with the fresh chilli and the remaining garlic, then toast for 1–2 minutes on each side, until golden and crispy.

5 Arrange the bread in a large serving bowl, and pour the fish stew over it, placing the lobster on top. Serve immediately. Follow the guidelines on page 21 if you are unsure about eating a whole lobster for the first time.

Energy 610kcal/2557kJ; Protein 65.8g; Carbohydrate 34.8g, of which sugars 9.7g; Fat 23.9g, of which saturates 3.5g; Cholesterol 150mg; Calcium 137mg; Fibre 3.7g; Sodium 473mg.

SERVES 4

1 small live lobster, about 400g/14oz
120ml/4fl oz/½ cup extra virgin olive oil
1 onion, finely chopped
1 garlic clove, finely chopped,
    plus 1 garlic clove, halved
30ml/2 tbsp chopped fresh parsley
500g/1¼lb canned tomatoes, sieved/
    strained
1 dried red chilli, chopped
1.5kg/3¼lb mixed fish, cut into even
    chunks
4 thick slices coarse, crusty bread
1 fresh red chilli, halved
salt and ground black pepper

LOBSTER AND CRAB STEAMED IN BEER

This authentic Vietnamese dish looks more complicated than it actually is. Whether you steam the lobsters and crabs at the same time will depend on the size of your steamer. But as they don't take long to cook, it's easy to steam them in batches. Lemon grass, herbs and nam pla are added to the steaming broth to make a simple dipping sauce.

1 Before cooking, place the lobsters and crabs in the freezer for a couple of hours to render them unconscious. Kill the lobsters and crabs following the instructions on page 19 and 22 respectively. Place half the lobsters and crabs in a large steamer and pour the beer into the base.

2 Scatter half the spring onions, ginger, chillies, lemon grass and herbs over the lobsters and crabs, and steam half the lobster and crabs for about 10 minutes, or until the lobsters turn red. Lift them on to a serving dish. Cook the rest of the lobsters and crabs in the same way.

3 Add the remaining lemon grass, herbs and nam pla to the simmering beer, stir in the lemon juice, then pour into a dipping bowl.

4 Serve the shellfish hot, dipping the lobster and crab meat into the beer broth and adding extra splashes of nam pla, if you like.

SERVES 4
4 live lobsters, about 450g/1lb each
4–8 live crabs, about 225g/8oz each
600ml/1 pint/2½ cups beer
4 spring onions/scallions, trimmed and chopped into long pieces
4cm/1½in fresh root ginger, peeled and finely sliced
2 green or red Thai chillies, seeded and finely sliced
3 lemon grass stalks, finely sliced
1 bunch of fresh dill, fronds chopped
1 bunch each of fresh basil and coriander/cilantro, stalks removed, leaves chopped
about 30ml/2 tbsp Thai fish sauce (nam pla), plus extra for serving
juice of 1 lemon
salt and ground black pepper

per portion: Energy 264Kcal/1112kJ; Protein 48g; Carbohydrate 4g, of which sugars 1g; Fat 7g, of which saturates 1g; Cholesterol 210mg; Calcium 185mg; Fibre 0.5g; Sodium 130g.

ZARZUELA

The word zarzuela means musical comedy in Spanish and this classic fish stew that is of the same name should be as lively and as colourful as the musical. This feast of fish includes lobster and other shellfish, but you can modify the ingredients to suit the occasion and availability. Serve with warmed chunks of bread for dipping.

SERVES 6
600g/1lb 6oz cooked lobster in its shell
24 live mussels or clams
1 large monkfish tail
225g/8oz squid rings
15ml/1 tbsp plain/all-purpose flour
90ml/6 tbsp olive oil
12 large raw prawns/shrimp, shelled
450g/1lb ripe tomatoes
2 large mild onions, chopped
4 garlic cloves, crushed
30ml/2 tbsp brandy
2 bay leaves
5ml/1 tsp paprika
1 red chilli, seeded and chopped
300ml/½ pint/1¼ cups fish stock
15g/½oz/2 tbsp ground almonds
30ml/2 tbsp chopped fresh parsley
salt and ground black pepper

1 Using a large knife, cut the lobster in half lengthways. Remove the dark intestine that runs down the length of the tail. Crack the claws using a hammer.

2 Scrub the mussels, discarding any that are damaged or open ones that do not close when tapped with a knife. Cut the monkfish fillets away from the central cartilage and cut each fillet into three.

3 Toss the monkfish and squid in seasoned flour. Heat the oil in a large frying pan. Add the monkfish and squid and fry quickly; remove from the pan. Fry the prawns on both sides, then remove from the pan.

4 Plunge the tomatoes into boiling water for 30 seconds, then refresh in cold water. Peel away the skins and chop roughly.

5 Add the onions and two-thirds of the garlic to the frying pan and fry for 3 minutes. Add the brandy and ignite with a taper. When the flames die down, add the tomatoes, bay leaves, paprika, chilli and stock.

6 Bring to the boil, reduce the heat and simmer gently for 5 minutes. Add the mussels or clams, cover and cook for 3–4 minutes, until the shells have opened. Remove the mussels or clams from the sauce and discard any that remain closed.

7 Arrange all the fish, including the lobster, in a large flameproof serving dish. Blend the ground almonds to a paste with the remaining garlic and parsley and stir into the sauce. Season with salt and pepper.

8 Pour the sauce over the fish and lobster and cook gently for about 5 minutes until hot. Serve immediately with plenty of warmed bread.

COOK'S TIP
For an easier-to-eat stew, remove all the meat from the lobster before adding it. Split it in two, down the middle, with a sharp knife. Remove the stomach sac from the head and the intestine tract, which runs down the tail. Remove the meat from the tail and the claws, taking care not to let it break up too much. Chop into large chunks and add to the stew as above. The cooked mussels can also be shelled and the meat added to the serving dish.

STEAMED SHELLFISH WITH TAMARIND DIP

This is one of the most popular shellfish dishes in the Philippines. The flavour-packed dip is made with tamarind, a long bean-shaped fruit which contains a sour pulp, which is usually processed to make a paste. It has a similar flavour to dates, but is not quite as sweet and is sometimes referred to as the Indian date. Serve with boiled rice.

SERVES 4–6

2 whole live lobsters, about 450g/1lb each

3–4 live crabs, about 225g/8oz each

24 live mussels or clams

24 raw king prawns/jumbo shrimp, with shells

6 spring onions/scallions, cut into 2.5cm/1in pieces and then into strips

6–8 black peppercorns

150ml/¼ pint/⅔ cup suka/Filipino coconut vinegar or rice vinegar

6 garlic cloves, crushed

about 50g/2oz fresh root ginger, finely sliced

24 fresh scallops (without shells)

lime wedges, to garnish

For the tamarind dip

2 limes

30ml/2 tbsp tamarind paste

2 spring onions/scallions, white parts only, finely chopped

2 red chillies, seeded and finely chopped

Energy 312kcal/1315kJ; Protein 61g; Carbohydrate 3.4g, of which sugars 0.5g; Fat 6.1g, of which saturates 1g; Cholesterol 309mg; Calcium 193mg; Fibre 0.6g; Sodium 769mg.

1 Before cooking, place the lobsters and crabs in the freezer for a couple of hours to render them unconscious. Kill the lobsters and crabs following the instructions on page 19 and 22 respectively.

2 Scrub the mussels or clams and prawns under cold running water, removing any beards, barnacles, and discarding any clams or mussels that are open and do not shut when sharply tapped.

3 Fill the bottom of two large steamers with at least 5cm/2in water, then divide the spring onions, peppercorns, suka vinegar, garlic and ginger between them. Cover and bring to the boil. Place the crab and lobster in the basket of one steamer and the small shellfish in the other. (You may need to steam them in batches, and top up the water when low.)

4 Cover the pans and steam the lobsters and crabs for 10 minutes and the mussels or clams, scallops and prawns for 5 minutes, until they turn opaque and the shells open. Discard any mussels or clams that have not opened. Remove the meat from the lobsters and crabs (see pages 20 and 22).

5 Meanwhile make the tamarind dip. Squeeze the juice from the limes and put in a small bowl. Add the tamarind paste and mix together. Add a little water to thin the mixture until it is of dipping consistency. Stir in the spring onions and chillies. Transfer to a small serving bowl.

6 Transfer the cooked shellfish to a warmed serving dish, garnish with lime wedges and serve with the dip, accompanied by rice.

VIETNAMESE STUFFED CRABS

SERVES 4

25g/1oz dried bean thread/cellophane noodles
6 dried cloud ear/wood ear mushrooms
450g/1lb cooked white or mixed white and brown crab meat
15ml/1 tbsp vegetable oil
10ml/2 tsp Thai fish sauce (nam pla)
2 shallots, finely chopped
2 garlic cloves, finely chopped
2.5cm/1in fresh root ginger, peeled and grated
1 small bunch of coriander/cilantro, stalks removed, leaves chopped
1 egg, beaten
25g/1oz/2 tbsp unsalted butter
salt and ground black pepper
fresh dill fronds, to garnish
sweet chilli sauce, to serve

In spite of the obvious French influence of stuffing shells and baking them, the Vietnamese have artfully made this dish their own with a combination of bean thread noodles and cloud ear mushrooms. Use freshly cooked crab meat from your fishmonger or supermarket if you wish, but you will also need four small, empty crab shells. Alternatively, use individual ovenproof dishes. Bean thread noodles and cloud ear mushrooms are available in Chinese and Asian markets.

1 Preheat the oven to 180°C/350°F/Gas 4. Soak the bean thread noodles and cloud ear mushrooms, separately, in bowls of lukewarm water, for 15 minutes. Squeeze them dry and chop them finely.

2 In a bowl, mix together the noodles and mushrooms with the crab meat. Add the oil, fish sauce, shallots, garlic, ginger and coriander. Season, then stir in the egg and mix in well.

3 Spoon the mixture into four small crab shells or individual ovenproof dishes, packing it in tightly, and dot the top of each one with a little butter.

4 Place the shells on a baking tray and cook for about 20 minutes, or until the tops are nicely browned. Garnish with dill and serve with a little sweet chilli sauce to drizzle over the top.

Nutritional information per portion: Energy 289Kcal/1206kJ; Protein 26g; Carbohydrate 8g, of which sugars 2g; Fat 17g, of which saturates 5g; Cholesterol 145mg; Calcium 39mg; Fibre 2.4g; Sodium 80g.

SEAFOOD IN PUFF PASTRY

The classic combination of seafood, including ready-cooked lobster, in a rich and creamy wine sauce served in a puff pastry case is found on the menus of many elegant restaurants in France.

SERVES 6

350g/12oz rough puff or puff pastry

1 egg beaten with 15ml/1 tbsp water, to glaze

60ml/4 tbsp dry white wine

2 shallots, finely chopped

450g/1lb live mussels, scrubbed and debearded

15g/½oz/1 tbsp unsalted butter

450g/1lb shelled scallops, cut in half crossways

450g/1lb raw king prawns/jumbo shrimp, shelled but with tails intact

175g/6oz cooked lobster meat, sliced

For the sauce

225g/8oz/1 cup unsalted butter, diced

2 shallots, finely chopped

250ml/8fl oz/1 cup fish stock

90ml/6 tbsp dry white wine

15–30ml/1–2 tbsp double/heavy cream

lemon juice, to taste

salt and white pepper

fresh dill sprigs, to garnish

1 Lightly grease a large baking sheet and sprinkle with a little water. On a lightly floured surface, roll out the pastry into a rectangle slightly less than 5mm/¼in thick. Using a sharp knife, cut into six diamond shapes about 12.5cm/5in long. Transfer to the baking sheet. Brush the pastry with egg glaze. Using the tip of a knife, score a line 1cm/½in from the edge, then lightly mark the centre in a criss-cross pattern.

2 Chill the pastry cases for 30 minutes. Preheat the oven to 220°C/425°F/Gas 7. Bake for about 20 minutes until puffed and golden. Transfer to a wire rack and, while still hot, remove each lid, cutting along the scored line to free it. Scoop out any uncooked dough from the middle and discard, then leave to cool.

3 In a large pan, bring the wine and shallots to the boil over a high heat. Add the mussels to the pan and cook, tightly covered, for 4–6 minutes until the shells open. Discard any mussels that do not open. Reserve 6 mussels for the garnish, then remove the rest from their shells and set aside in a bowl. Strain the cooking liquid through a muslin-lined sieve or strainer and reserve for the sauce.

4 In a heavy frying pan, melt the butter over a medium heat. Add the scallops and prawns, cover tightly and cook for 3–4 minutes, shaking and stirring occasionally, until they feel just firm to the touch; do not overcook. Using a slotted spoon, transfer the scallops and prawns to the bowl with the mussels and add any cooking juices to the mussel liquid.

5 To make the sauce, melt 25g/1oz of the butter in a heavy pan. Add the shallots and cook for 2 minutes. Pour in the fish stock and boil for about 15 minutes over a high heat until reduced by three-quarters. Add the white wine and reserved mussel liquid and boil for 5–7 minutes until reduced by half. Lower the heat to medium and whisk in the remaining butter, a little at a time, to make a smooth thick sauce (do not allow it to boil). Whisk in the cream and season with salt, if needed, pepper and lemon juice. Cover and keep warm.

6 Warm the pastry cases in a low oven for about 10 minutes. Put the mussels, scallops and prawns in a large pan. Stir in a quarter of the sauce and reheat over a low heat. Gently stir in the lobster meat and warm for a further minute.

7 Arrange the pastry case bases on individual plates. Divide the seafood mixture equally among them and top with the lids. Garnish each with a mussel and a dill sprig and spoon the remaining sauce around the edges, or serve separately.

Energy 750kcal/3147kJ; Protein 48.1g; Carbohydrate 26g, of which sugars 1.2g; Fat 49g, of which saturates 27.5g; Cholesterol 361mg; Calcium 162mg; Fibre 0.1g; Sodium 717mg.

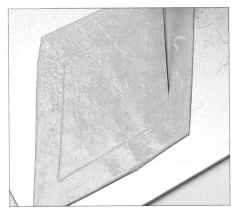

SINGAPORE CHILLI CRAB

This could be described as Singapore's signature dish; it's a favourite street food and steaming woks of deep-frying crab are a common sight at stalls and coffee shops. To serve, the crabs are placed in the centre of the table, the shells are carefully cracked open, and the meat is dipped into the cooking sauce.

SERVES 4

4 live crabs, about 250g/9oz each
vegetable oil, for deep-frying
30ml/2 tbsp sesame oil
30–45ml/2–3 tbsp chilli sauce
45ml/3 tbsp tomato ketchup
15ml/1 tbsp soy sauce
15ml/1 tbsp sugar
250ml/8fl oz/1 cup chicken stock
   or water
2 eggs, beaten
salt and ground black pepper
2 spring onions/scallions, finely sliced,
   and fresh coriander/cilantro leaves,
   finely chopped, to garnish

For the spice paste

4 garlic cloves, chopped
25g/1oz fresh root ginger, chopped
4 red chillies, seeded and chopped

1 Prepare the crab. To chop a crab in half, killing it instantly, lay it on its back and position a cleaver down the centre line, then strike the back of the cleaver with a mallet. Or follow the instructions on page 22 for freezing and boiling, but boil for just 5 minutes before removing from the water, so they are not quite cooked.

2 Using a mortar and pestle or food processor, grind the ingredients for the spice paste and set aside.

3 Heat enough oil for deep-frying in a wok or heavy pan. Drop in the crabs and fry until the shells turn bright red. Remove from the oil and drain. Cool, remove the claws and legs and halve the bodies if boiled.

4 Heat the sesame oil in a wok and stir in the spice paste. Fry the paste until fragrant then stir in the chilli sauce, ketchup, soy sauce and sugar.

5 Toss in the fried crab and coat well in the sauce. Pour in the chicken stock or water and bring to the boil. Reduce the heat and simmer for 5 minutes. Season the sauce to taste.

6 Pour in the eggs, stirring gently, to let them set in the sauce. Serve immediately, garnished with spring onions and fresh coriander.

Energy 115kcal/481kJ; Protein 21.7g; Carbohydrate 1.1g, of which sugars 0.9g; Fat 1.8g, of which saturates 3.1g; Cholesterol 126mg; Calcium 23mg; Fibre 0.3g; Sodium 674mg.

BAKED CRAB GRATIN

SERVES 6

6 live crabs, about 250g/9oz each
350ml/12fl oz/1½ cups beer
115g/4oz/1 cup coarse sea salt
10ml/2 tsp sugar
40g/1½oz/¼ cup Cheddar cheese,
  grated

For the sauce
25g/1oz/2 tbsp unsalted butter
15ml/1 tbsp plain/all-purpose flour
475ml/16fl oz/2 cups double/heavy
  cream
2 egg yolks
30ml/2 tbsp brandy
10ml/2 tsp liquid from a can of
  anchovies, or other fish stock
salt and ground black pepper

This is a rich and indulgent dish, with a moreish cream and brandy sauce. Leaving the cooked crabs in their poaching liquid overnight gives the flesh extra flavour.

1 Follow the instructions for killing live crabs on page 22. Put 3 litres/5 pints/12 cups water, the beer, salt and sugar in a very large pan and bring to the boil. Drop the crabs in, two at a time, and cook for 15 minutes. Remove the crabs from the water and transfer to a large bowl. Repeat with the remaining crabs.

2 Pour the hot cooking liquid over the crabs, cool, and then leave in the refrigerator overnight. Remove the crabs from the liquid and reserve 300ml/½ pint/1¼ cups. Extract the meat from the crabs (reserving the shells) following the instructions on pages 22–23. Preheat the oven to 200°C/400°F/Gas 6.

3 To make the sauce, melt the butter in a pan, add the flour and cook over a low heat for 1 minute, stirring to make a roux. Remove from the heat and slowly add the reserved liquid, stirring all the time, to form a smooth sauce.

4 Return to the heat and cook, stirring, for 2–3 minutes until the sauce boils and thickens. Remove from the heat, stir in the cream then add the egg yolks, brandy and anchovy liquid and season to taste with salt and pepper.

5 Add the extracted crab meat to the sauce and then put the mixture into the empty crab shells. Sprinkle the grated Cheddar cheese on top and bake in the oven for 10–15 minutes until the crab meat mixture is golden brown. Serve hot.

Energy 544kcal/2244kJ; Protein 10.9g; Carbohydrate 6.1g, of which sugars 4.2g; Fat 51.7g, of which saturates 30.8g; Cholesterol 209mg; Calcium 112mg; Fibre 0.1g; Sodium 216mg.

CRAYFISH IN DILL

Eating crayfish in early autumn is almost a sacred ritual in Sweden and Finland as traditionally crayfish harvesting ended at the end of the summer. This dish is eaten as a celebration with copious amounts of schnapps and beer.

SERVES 6–8

2kg/4½lb live crayfish

100g/4oz/1 cup coarse sea salt

10ml/2 tsp sugar

1 large bunch dill flowers (available from florists in the summer season or use fresh dill and dill seeds to infuse the crayfish with a similar flavour), plus extra dill, to garnish

1 onion, chopped

350ml/12fl oz/1½ cups stout/dark beer

fresh dill, to garnish

mature/sharp Cheddar cheese and toasted bread, to serve

COOK'S TIP

Live crayfish should be purged before cooking; see page 23 for instructions.

Energy 115kcal/481kJ; Protein 21.7g; Carbohydrate 1.1g, of which sugars 0.9g; Fat 1.8g, of which saturates 0.5g; Cholesterol 78mg; Calcium 141mg; Fibre 0.1g; Sodium 1527mg.

1 Put the crayfish in strong plastic bags, about 10–15 per bag, seal and place in the freezer for 2 hours to render them unconscious.

2 Put 3 litres/5 pints/12 cups water, salt and sugar in a large pan and bring to the boil. Put the dill flowers, or dill and dill seeds, in a large bowl and add the onion and stout.

3 Remove the crayfish from the freezer, unseal a bag and drop 10–15 crayfish into the boiling water. Cover the pan, return to the boil and cook for about 8 minutes, until they turn a bright orange colour. Using a slotted spoon, remove the crayfish from the water and place on top of the dill. Repeat with the remaining crayfish until they are all cooked.

4 Pour the hot cooking liquid over the cooked crayfish in the bowl and allow to cool in the liquid, then leave to marinate in the refrigerator overnight to infuse. Serve the crayfish the following day, garnished with fresh dill and accompanied by cheese and toast.

INDEX

American lobsters 10
asparagus
   crab and asparagus soup
      with nuoc cham 44
   dressed crab with
      asparagus 71
avocados
   citrus lobster wraps 66

banana leaves
   spiced lobster in banana
      leaf 94
barbecue racks 17
basil
   grilled lobster with basil
      mayonnaise 103
   lobster and crab steamed in
      beer 112
beef
   king prawns and beef
      oriental salad 58
   surf and turf burgers 68–9
beer
   lobster and crab steamed in
      beer 112
beetroot
   crab, horseradish and
      beetroot salad 70
beurre blanc 26
blue crabs 12
   blue crab soup 46
brandy
   drunken prawns 56
   lobster bisque 32
   lobster thermidor 96

brioche buns
   hot lobster brioche rolls 65
   surf and turf burgers 68–9
brown crabs 12
brown shrimp 14
butter and herb sauce 27
butternut squash
   crayfish chowder 37

California crabs 12
Canadian lobsters 10
capelli d'angelo with lobster
   78
cappucino of lobster, Puy
   lentils and tarragon 45
cheese
   baked crab gratin 124
   crab and ricotta tartlets 54
   creamy crab bake 53
chilli
   crab and chilli soup with
      fresh coriander relish 39
   hot and spicy crab claws 55
   peri-peri crawfish 100–1
   Singapore chilli crab 123
citrus lobster wraps 66
citrus salsa, fiery 28
clams
   chunky seafood chupe 41
   steamed shellfish with
      tamarind dip 116
   zarzuela 114
cleavers 16
coconut
   lobster, coconut and
      coriander soup 34
common edible crabs 12
common prawns 14
common shrimp 14
coral (roe) 20
coriander
   crab and chilli soup with
      fresh coriander relish 39
   lobster, coconut and
      coriander soup 34
corn
   corn and crab soup 42
   crayfish chowder 37

crab 12–13
   baked crab gratin 124
   blue crab soup 46
   buying crab 18–19
   cooking crab 13, 22
   corn and crab soup 42
   crab and asparagus soup
      with nuoc cham 44
   crab and chilli soup with
      fresh coriander relish 39
   crab meat salad with garlic
      dressing 72
   crab soup 40
   crab with mushrooms and
      noodles 88
   crab, horseradish and
      beetroot salad 70
   creamy crab bake 53
   dressed crab with
      asparagus 71
   hot and spicy crab claws 55
   linguine with crab 87
   lobster and crab steamed in
      beer 112
   preparing 22
   removing meat from a
      cooked crab 22–3
   Singapore chilli crab 123
   steamed shellfish with
      tamarind dip 116
   storing crab 19
   Vietnamese stuffed crabs
      119
crawfish 11
   peri-peri crawfish 100–1
crayfish 15
   cooking crayfish 15
   crayfish chowder 37
   crayfish in dill 125
   crayfish sauce 27
   shelling cooked crayfish 25
cream
   creamy lobster soup 33
   Dublin lawyer 52
   grilled lobster with
      tarragon cream 92
   lobster ravioli 76
   lobster thermidor 96

lobster with wholegrain
   mustard and cream 99
cucumber
   crab meat salad with garlic
      dressing 72

deep-sea prawns 14
dill
   crayfish in dill 125
drunken prawns 56
Dublin Bay prawns 15, 83
Dublin lawyer 52
Dungeness crabs 12

equipment 16–17
European lobsters 10–11

fish
   Sardinian fish stew with
      lobster 110

garlic
   crab meat salad with garlic
      dressing 72
ginger
   lobster and crab steamed in
      beer 112
Gulf prawns/ shrimp 14

hollandaise sauce 26
horseradish
   crab, horseradish and
      beetroot salad 70

Japanese prawns 14
jumbo shrimp 14

king crabs 12–13
king prawns 14
   barbecued king prawns
      105
   drunken prawns 56
   king prawns and beef
      oriental salad 58
   king prawns in crispy batter
      57
   prawns with lemon grass
      107

satay prawns 106
seafood in puff pastry 120
steamed shellfish with
    tamarind dip 116
kuruma prawns 14

langoustines 15
    cooking langoustines 15
    shelling cooked
    langoustines 24
    steamed langoustines with
    lemon grass risotto 83
lemon and lime sauce 28
lemon grass
    prawns with lemon grass
    107
    steamed langoustines with
    lemon grass risotto 83
lentils
    cappucino of lobster, Puy
    lentils and tarragon 45
linguine with crab 87
lobster 8–10
    barbecuing lobster 20
    buying lobster 18–19
    capelli d'angelo with
    lobster 78
    cappucino of lobster, Puy
    lentils and tarragon 45
    citrus lobster wraps 66
    cold water lobsters 10–11
    cooking lobster 11, 19
    creamy lobster soup 33
    Dublin lawyer 52
    eating a whole lobster 21
    grilled lobster with basil
    mayonnaise 103
    grilled lobster with
    tarragon cream 92
    grilling lobster
    hot lobster brioche rolls
    65
    lobster and crab steamed in
    beer 112
    lobster and filo tart 54
    lobster and tomato soup
    36
    lobster bisque 32

lobster cakes with tartare
    sauce 51
lobster noodles 80
lobster ravioli 76
lobster stock 21
lobster thermidor 96
lobster with wholegrain
    mustard and cream 99
lobster, coconut and
    coriander soup 34
oven-baked lobster and
    spinach risotto 84
potted lobster 50
preparing lobster 19
removing meat from a
    cooked lobster 20
Sardinian fish stew with
    lobster 110
seafood in puff pastry 120
spiced lobster in banana
    leaf 94
steamed lobster tails 29
steamed shellfish with
    tamarind dip 116
storing lobster 19
surf and turf burgers 68–9
truffle and lobster risotto
    79
warm baby new potato and
    lobster salad 62–3
warm water lobsters 11
zarzuela 114
lobster crackers 16
lobster picks 16

mallets 17
mayonnaise, never-fail 26
    grilled lobster with basil
    mayonnaise 103
Mediterranean prawns 14
monkfish
    zarzuela 114
mushrooms
    crab with mushrooms and
    noodles 88
    lobster ravioli 76
mussels
    chunky seafood chupe 41

seafood in puff pastry 120
steamed shellfish with
    tamarind dip 116
zarzuela 114
mustard
    crab meat salad with garlic
    dressing 72
    creamy crab bake 53
    lobster with wholegrain
    mustard and cream 99

noodles
    crab with mushrooms and
    noodles 88
    lobster noodles 80
    stir-fried prawns with rice
    noodles 89
Norway lobster 15
nuoc cham
    crab and asparagus soup
    with nuoc cham 44

pans 16–17
pasta
    capelli d'angelo with
    lobster 78
    linguine with crab 87
    lobster ravioli 76
pear
    crab meat salad with garlic
    dressing 72
peppers
    citrus lobster wraps 66
peri-peri crawfish 100–1
potatoes
    crayfish chowder 37
    warm baby new potato and
    lobster salad 62–3
pots 16–17
potted lobster 50
potted shrimps 25
poultry shears 16
prawns 14
    barbecued king prawns
    105
    buying prawns 23
    chunky seafood chupe 41
    cooking prawns 14

drunken prawns 56
fantail prawns 24
griddled tiger prawns 104
grilling large prawns on the
    barbecue 24
king prawns and beef
lobster and filo tart 54
oriental salad 58
king prawns in crispy batter
    57
peeling and deveining raw
    prawns 23
poaching prawns 23
prawns with lemon grass
    107
satay prawns 106
seafood in puff pastry 120
shelling cooked prawns 24
steamed shellfish with
    tamarind dip 116
stir-fried prawns with rice
    noodles 89
storing and purging 23
zarzuela 114

ravioli, lobster 76
rice
    oven-baked lobster and
    spinach risotto 84
    steamed langoustines with
    lemon grass risotto 83
    truffle and lobster risotto
    79
roasting tins 17

satay prawns 106
sauces for shellfish 26–8
scallops
   chunky seafood chupe 41
   seafood in puff pastry 120
   steamed shellfish with
     tamarind dip 116
scampi 15
shrimp 14
   potted shrimps 25
   stir-fried prawns with rice
     noodles 89
Singapore chilli crab 123
slipper lobsters 11
snow crabs 13
spiced lobster in banana leaf
   94
spider crabs 13
spinach
   oven-baked lobster and
     spinach risotto 84
squat lobsters 11
squid
   chunky seafood chupe 41
   zarzuela 114
stone crabs 13
surf and turf burgers 68–9
swimming crabs 13

tamarind
   steamed shellfish with
     tamarind dip 116
tarragon
   cappucino of lobster, Puy
     lentils and tarragon 45
   grilled lobster with tarragon
     cream 92
tartare sauce
   green tartare sauce 28
   lobster cakes with tartare
     sauce 51
tiger prawns 14
   griddled tiger prawns 104
tomalley 20, 101
tomatoes
   linguine with crab 87
   lobster and tomato soup 36
   Sardinian fish stew with
     lobster 110
truffle and lobster risotto
   79

Vietnamese stuffed crabs
   119

whiskey
   Dublin lawyer 52

yabby 15
yogurt
   citrus lobster wraps 66

This edition is published by Lorenz Books,
an imprint of Anness Publishing Ltd, 108 Great Russell Street,
London WC1B 3NA. email: info@anness.com
www.annesspublishing.com   twitter: @Anness_Books

© Anness Publishing Limited 2016

Publisher: Joanna Lorenz
Editor: Helen Sudell
Designer: Adelle Morris
Special Photography: David Griffen
Production Controller: Ben Worley

A CIP catalogue record for this book is available from the British Library

If you like the images in this book and would like to investigate using them
for publishing, promotions or advertising, please visit our website
www.practicalpictures.com for more information.

PUBLISHER'S NOTE
Although the advice and information in this book are believed to be accurate and
true at the time of going to press, neither the authors nor the publisher can accept
any legal responsibility or liability for any errors or omissions that may have been
made nor for any inaccuracies nor for any loss, harm or injury that comes about
from following instructions or advice in this book.

PICTURE ACKNOWLEDGMENTS
Istock: p9; p10bl; p11; p15bl and br; p17br; p21tl; p42tl; p48; p60; p74; p76;
p93bl; p108; p109bl and tr; p110tl.

COOK'S NOTES
For all recipes, quantities are given in both metric and imperial measures and, where
appropriate, in standard cups and spoons. Follow one set of measures, but not a
mixture, because they are not interchangeable.

Standard spoon and cup measures are level. 1 tsp = 5ml, 1 tbsp = 15ml, 1 cup =
250ml/8fl oz. Australian standard tablespoons are 20ml. Australian readers should
use 3 tsp in place of
1 tbsp for measuring small quantities.

American pints are 16fl oz/2 cups. American readers should use 20fl oz/2.5 cups in
place of 1 pint when measuring liquids.

Electric oven temperatures in this book are for conventional ovens. When using a fan
oven, the temperature will need to be reduced by about 10–20°C/20–40°F. Since
ovens vary, you should check with your manufacturer's instruction book for guidance.

The nutritional analysis given for each recipe is calculated per portion (i.e. serving
or item), unless otherwise stated. If the recipe gives a range, such as Serves 4–6,
then the nutritional analysis will be for the smaller portion size, i.e. 6 servings. The
analysis does not include optional ingredients, such as garnishes or salt added to
taste.

Medium (US large) eggs are used unless otherwise stated.

SUSTAINABLE FISH STOCKS
Try to check that the lobster or other shellfish you buy is from a sustainable
source – the Marine Stewardship Council has useful information on worldwide
stockists at www.msc.org.

CERTIFIED
SUSTAINABLE
SEAFOOD
MSC
www.msc.org